HOW BETTER REGULATION CAN SHAPE THE FUTURE OF INDONESIA'S ELECTRICITY SECTOR

DECEMBER 2020

ADB

ASIAN DEVELOPMENT BANK

© 2020 Asian Development Bank
6 ADB Avenue, Mandaluyong City, 1550 Metro Manila, Philippines
Tel +63 2 8632 4444; Fax +63 2 8636 2444
www.adb.org

Some rights reserved. Published in 2020.

ISBN 978-92-9262-657-0 (print); 978-92-9262-658-7 (electronic); 978-92-9262-659-4 (ebook)
Publication Stock No. TCS200427
DOI: http://dx.doi.org/10.22617/TCS200427

Corrigenda to ADB publications may be found at http://www.adb.org/publications/corrigenda.

Note:
In this publication, "$" refers to United States dollars.

Cover design by Jan Carlo dela Cruz.

This report was prepared by PT. Castlerock and Economic Consulting Associates for the Ministry of Finance of Indonesia.

Contents

Tables, Figures, and Boxes

Abbreviations

ADB	Asian Development Bank
AMDAL	Analisis Mengenai Dampak Lingkungan (Environmental Impact Analysis)
ANEEL	Agência Nacional de Energia Elétrica (National Electric Energy Agency)
BAPPENAS	Badan Perencanaan dan Pembangunan Nasional (National Development Planning Agency)
BKPM	Badan Koordinasi Penanaman Modal (Investment Coordinating Board)
BPJT	Badan Pengaturan Jalan Tol (Indonesia Toll Road Authority)
BP MIGAS	Badan Pelaksana Kegiatan Usaha Hulu Minyak dan Gas Bumi (Oil and Gas Upstream Business Activities Operational Agency)
BPPTL	Badan Pengawas Pasar Tenaga Listrik (Electricity Market Supervisory Agency)
BPS	Badan Pusat Statistik (Statistics Indonesia)
BPPT	Badan Pengkajian dan Penerapan Teknologi (Agency for the Assessment and Application of Technology)
BRTI	Badan Regulasi Telekomunikasi Indonesia (Indonesian Telecommunication Regulatory Body)
CAPEX	capital expenses
CMEA	Kementerian Koordinator Bidang Perekonomian (Coordinating Ministry for Economic Affairs)
DPR	Dewan Perwakilan Rakyat (House of Representatives)
DPRD	Dewan Perwakilan Rakyat Daerah (Regional House of Representatives)
EPE	Empresa de Pesquisa Energética (Energy Research Office)
ERO	Kosovo Energy Regulatory Service
ESA	electricity sales agent
IIGF	PT Penjaminan Infrastruktur Indonesia (Indonesian Infrastructure Guarantee Fund)
IPP	Independent Power Producer
IPPPP	Independent Power Producers Procurement Programme
IRP	Integrated Resource Plan
ISO	independent system operator
IUPTL	Izin Usaha Penyediaan Tenaga Listrik (Electricity Supply Business Permit)
KPPIP	Komite Percepatan Penyediaan Infrastruktur Prioritas (The Committee for the Acceleration of Prioritized Infrastructure Development)
KSP	Kantor Staff Presiden (Presidential Staff Office)
MA	Mahkamah Agung (Supreme Court)
MEF	Kementerian Lingkungan Hidup dan Kehutanan (Ministry of Environment and Forestry)

MOCI	Kementerian Komunikasi dan Informatika (Ministry of Communication and Informatics)
MOF	Kementerian Keuangan (Ministry of Finance)
MOPWH	Kementerian Pekerjaan Umum dan Perumahan Rakyat (Ministry of Public Works and Housing)
MEMR	Kementerian Energi dan Sumber Daya Mineral (Ministry of Energy and Mineral Resources)
MK	Mahkamah Konstitusi (Constitutional Court)
MWh	megawatt-hour
NERC	Nigerian Electricity Regulatory Commission
OECD	Organisation for Economic Co-operation and Development
OPEX	operational expenses
OSS	Online Single Submission
PKLN	Pengelolaan Pinjaman Komersial Luar Negeri (Overseas Commercial Loan Management Coordination)
PLN	Perusahaan Perseroan (Persero) PT Perusahaan Listrik Negara (State Electricity Company)
PPA	power purchase agreement
PSC	Production Sharing Contract
PWC	PricewaterhouseCoopers
RUKD	Rencana Umum Ketenagalistrikan Daerah (Regional Electricity Plan)
RUKN	Rencana Umum Ketenagalistrikan Nasional (National Electricity Plan)
RUPTL	Rencana Usaha Penyediaan Tenaga Listrik (Electricity Supply Business Plan)
SKK Migas	Satuan Kerja Khusus Pelaksana Kegiatan Usaha Hulu Minyak dan Gas Bumi (Special Task Force for Upstream Oil and Gas Business Activities)
SKS	Satuan Kerja Sementara (Temporary Working Operational Unit)
PT SMI	Sarana Multi Infrastruktur
SOE	state-owned enterprise
T&D	transmission and distribution
TNDP	transmission network development plan
TSO	transmission system operator
TWh	terawatt-hours
UK	United Kingdom
US	United States

Acknowledgments

The Indonesian National Development Agency - Badan Perencanaan Pembangunan Nasional (BAPPENAS) and the Asian Development Bank (ADB) prepared this publication under the Sustainable Infrastructure Assistance Program - Technical Assistance 9511, funded by the Government of Australia's Department of Foreign Affairs and Trade and under the guidance and leadership of the Ministry of National Development Planning of the Republic of Indonesia's Directorate of Energy, Telecommunication and Informatics.

Florian Kitt, Energy Specialist, Southeast Energy Sector Department, led the TA team. Dennis Volk, Deputy Director, Bundesnetzagentur, Kirana Sastrawijaya, Senior Partner, Umbra Law, and Faela Sufa, ADB Consultant undertook the research and initial write-up. Michael Crosetti, Managing Director, Castle Rock Consulting, provided inputs and reviewed the analysis.

Jeffrey Almera provided administrative assistance while the team from Department of Communications provided editorial, and production support.

The following energy officers from ADB's knowledge departments and operations departments provided inputs, insights into operations, and comments on the study: Yongping Zhai, Toru Kubo, and Kee-Yung Nam.

Summary and Recommendations

The current regulatory framework on electricity in Indonesia is provided under Law No. 30 of 2009 on Electricity (the 2009 Electricity Law). Regulations are implemented by a number of ministries such as the Ministry of Energy and Mineral Resources (MEMR), the Ministry of Industry, the Ministry of Finance (MOF), the Ministry of Environment and Forestry, and others with relevant responsibilities relating to electricity sector. The MEMR currently acts as the regulator to the Indonesian electricity sector, which is served by a vertically integrated company—the State Electricity Company (PLN)—and a degree of private sector participation.

Our situational analysis and review of stakeholder opinions in Indonesia strongly indicates that the current decision-making structures do not serve the Indonesian electricity sector well. With the MEMR currently acting as the Indonesian electricity regulator, policy formulation and implementation are centralized in one institution. This structure can promote suboptimal regulatory decisions originating from conflicts of interest, as the ministry is both holder of economic and political interests and regulator. In consequence, key processes for the Indonesian electricity sector fail to deliver efficient overall sector performance. These processes include the determination of electricity tariffs, approval of long-term investment plans, and the procurement of infrastructure.

Tariff determination does not reflect true economic costs and can further result in misallocated costs among customer groups. These conditions seem to result in tariff-based revenue streams that impede PLN to fully recover its investments. Financial support from the MOF to bridge PLN's financial gap has declined since 2012. More recently this trend is reversing with an anticipated growth in the future. A tariff increase is widely considered as the only option left.

PLN-led investment planning currently lacks alignment with policy objectives (such as least cost), transparency, and enforcement. As such, investment plans fail to attract timely and efficient investment from PLN as well as strategic engagement by third party investors (e.g., local banks, independent power producers, and international financial institutions).

PLN-led infrastructure procurement currently lacks transparency, oversight, and enforcement. This results in PLN (being perceived as) having too much market power resulting from its dominant position as single buyer and main generation asset owner in the Indonesian market.

The shortcomings warrant improvements to the abovementioned processes. In this context, global experience strongly suggests the benefits of a dedicated regulatory body in the Indonesian electricity sector. A dedicated electricity regulatory body would be an important new player in Indonesia's institutional electricity landscape similar to other sector regulators. If empowered to take high-quality decisions in the context of the abovementioned processes, the regulator can significantly contribute to achieving Indonesia's sector targets. At the same time, it can build and maintain market participants' confidence and ensure acceptance from all stakeholders. Embedded into a sound governance framework, and equipped with decision-making competence, a regulator will function as a "referee" for the Indonesian electricity sector.

The following brief description of stakeholders' considerations in the context of infrastructure planning may serve as an example for the benefits of good regulatory decision-making: government, investors, and consumers all look at infrastructure plans with different considerations in mind. While it will be challenging to satisfy all interests at the same time and level, a regulator can establish evidence-based decisions that maximize societal benefits while ensuring buy-in and acceptance.

- Governments are predominantly concerned about congruency of established policy targets with the plans' outcomes (e.g., Will the planned and developed assets ensure supply of electricity at a targeted reliability level? Does the plan deliver on an established share of renewables in the electricity system?) as well as wider acceptance of and ability to implement the plan (in time).

- Investors look at infrastructure plans with a view to assess the implications on the existing assets they hold as well as on the impact on their individual future business opportunities, which can be influenced by technology knowledge, risk profiles, and available risk mitigation instruments.

- Consumers and other stakeholders (e.g., environmental groups) are mostly concerned about quality of supply at least cost when considering all technology alternatives, and also the congruency of the plan's outcomes with societal and environmental norms and expectations (e.g., Will the plan deliver local jobs? Does the plan create long-time liabilities to society or the environment?). A subset of consumers will also expect to influence locational choices and infrastructure alternatives in preparation for infrastructure siting.

A regulatory body in Indonesia electricity is not a new idea. In 2002, the Indonesian government introduced the Electricity Market Supervisory Agency (BPPTL) through the issuance of Law No. 20 of 2002 on Electricity (2002 Electricity Law). This agency had the authority and responsibility in making independent decisions to carry out the regulation and supervision of electricity supply in the areas where competition applies. However, in December 2004, the Constitutional Court of Indonesia (MK) ruled the 2002 Electricity Law to be unconstitutional on the basis that it contravened Article 33 of the 1945 Indonesian Constitution, which was interpreted to require that the state has control over the electricity sector. Furthermore, with the revocation of the 2002 Electricity Law, BPPTL was dissolved. The MK ruling was based on the reasoning that the aim of the 2002 Electricity Law was to unbundle the electricity market, which MK considered not in accordance with the values of Indonesian economics. MK argued that the law failed to meet the five principles for Indonesia's minimum standard of state control in the energy sector as introduced by MK: policy, action, regulation, management, and supervision.

The establishment of a new independent regulatory body in the electricity sector requires careful management of such an organization along the lines of the five principles. These constitutional requirements to maintain state control over the Indonesian electricity sector ultimately affect the structures in which a regulatory body would be able to operate, its staffing, and its decision-making competence.

With the correct legal rationalization of state control principles, there is no insurmountable constitutional or legal barrier to introduce an electricity regulatory body in Indonesia. We conclude that the establishment of an Indonesian electricity regulatory body does not necessarily mean that the government's power to exercise "state control" would be undermined.

The study recommends that Indonesia implement a regulatory body for the electricity sector, to be governed in a way that results in high-quality decisions. Among other requirements, this body needs clarity on its role, prevention against undue influence, and neutral funding sources. We recommend establishing a structure within the body that fosters evidence-based decision-making while retaining the control from the state over the regulator's activities. Enhanced transparency will be key to the integrity of its decisions.

The study suggests establishing the regulatory body through the issuance of a government or presidential regulation. A ministerial regulation does not appear to have the sufficient force required to establish a new organization and could set a too direct and close relationship between the regulatory body's intended actions and the ministry's rights to approve these actions. The ultimate decision whether to establish the regulatory body by government regulation or presidential regulation will have to consider the speed and simplicity of the approach, as well as the reliability of the legal arrangement. To deliver high-quality regulatory decisions in the long run, the government of Indonesia should implement a law to establish the regulator. While implementation of the law will require time, a temporary presidential regulation may be used to expedite the process.

The government needs to decide whether the regulator is to be established as a directorate within MEMR or as a separate governmental organization with MEMR to provide oversight over the regulator's actions relative to the implementation of government policy. The study finds that the regulator should ideally be established as a separate government organization. Establishing the regulator along the lines of best practice governance frameworks will result in a trustworthy regulator under MEMR supervision. The benefits of a separate governmental organization will arise from stakeholders' stronger perception of integrity. Funding for the regulator would become more transparent with a separate budget line from the government, instead of relying on MEMR to set and administer the regulator's budget.

The scope and depth of cooperation with other stakeholders needs to be established, e.g., for the Indonesian regulator to seek approval by the government and House of Representatives (DPR) for setting retail electricity tariffs per the requirements of the 2009 Electricity Law.

Transparency rules are to be put in place, which should cover all relevant communication between the regulator, the political sphere, regulated entities, and other stakeholders. The government should retain the legal right to direct the regulator in its decisions, e.g. if the regulator failed to account for the incorporation of (a) specific political objective(s). The process to direct the regulator needs to increase transparency in order to strengthen the trust and acceptance of regulatory decisions and contribute to acceptance of deviation from decisions made beforehand on a political level.

An internal system of accountability should enable government to measure and assess the regulator's performance. In this context, annual performance reporting can support governmental oversight.

A funding framework for the regulator and its activities should support high-quality regulatory decision-making processes and maintain the regulator's neutrality. Simplicity and adequacy are as important as transparency of the source of the funding. To the extent legally possible, a mix of funding sources is suggested, including dedicated budget lines from either government or the budget from the MEMR (the latter under written agreement); regulatory fees; including income from penalties and fines and interest earned on investments and trust funds.

Building on a clearly defined set of tasks, the regulator should work within a clearly defined scope in coordination with the political sphere, but also within the institution. The latter aspect will define the membership composition and split in responsibilities between the regulator's governing body and the head of the institution (e.g., chief executive officer or president).

For day-to-day decision-making, the regulator can benefit from an internal governing board. Most relevant in this regard is to establish a board structure with multiple decision makers to ensure different experiences and perspectives are included in regulatory decision-making, and to enhance the institutional memory for tasks which require long-lasting involvement (such as tariff setting or investment planning). The governing bodies should consist of experts in their respective fields. To maintain information exchange and build trust in the regulator's decisions, representatives from the political sphere and/or MEMR could be invited as observers in meetings of the governing body. The more direct decision-making authority is given to the regulator (instead of an advisory role or the role to propose rulings to government), the less (perceived) notion of influence from the political sphere or the industry.

The independence of the staff of this new regulatory body matters as much as their level of expertise—key managerial positions and board members should only be filled with PLN staff or staff from MEMR when there are no alternatives. PLN and/or MEMR staff on loan is to be avoided in those positions to prevent conflict of interest. In this context, we suggest the presidential office to approve managerial candidates proposed by the regulator. Proposals for the chief executive officer level are recommended to be made by MEMR, with board members and below to be hired in-house through the regulator's human resource processes. The appointment for managerial positions is determined based on merit system, or based on qualifications, competencies, and performance, and is held in a transparent and competitive manner in accordance with good governance principles. If the employees in this regulatory body will be determined as government employees or *Aparatur Sipil Negara*, the selection process for certain positions must follow the existing framework, as regulated in Law No. 5/2014, on how the Government of Indonesia recruits its government employees. High-level staff, e.g., board members or senior agents, should not be involved in decisions related to previous employers, and the appointment and contract termination process for high-level staff should be explicitly stated in the rules for establishing the regulatory organization.

Assuming an initial lack of expert staff at the required scale, the regulator should initially focus on maintaining the integrity of the processes mentioned above and function more as a moderator between stakeholders and use outside knowledge for addressing specific questions. The regulator's managerial staff should strategically build in-house expertise in the required fields to allow for deeper regulatory oversight.

With initial introduction of the regulator, the regulator should be given clear roles, responsibilities, and enforcement powers in infrastructure planning, procurement, tariff setting, and electrification.

The regulator's role in investment planning should be to ensure alignment of the investment plan with policy objectives; enhance transparency on the data and models used; facilitate input from all stakeholders and ensure consideration of their input; identify an optimal investment portfolio for generation and transmission infrastructure based on PLN's draft investment plan; and approve the investment plan, including individual projects or suggest its approval to government.

The regulator's role in the procurement process should be to monitor and enforce the projects resulting from the investment plan; perform licensing tasks; define and supervise a selected (set of) competitive procurement models and processes, including bid evaluation, approval of power purchase agreement standards, and stakeholder complaint management; as well as project implementation prudence review and enforcement. The regulator should further ensure that costs associated from procured projects are being included in tariffs.

The regulator's role in the tariff-setting process should be to continuously identify true economic costs of the electricity supply industry, solicit input from all stakeholders, propose tariffs, and support political consensus-building among stakeholders through evidence-based assessments and contributions. In this context, the regulator should also identify target groups and methodologies to protect low-income consumers.

The regulator's role in electrification should be to ensure technical standards through licensing and registration for mini-grids; determine the least-cost means of electrifying unserved areas, e.g., by PLN grid extension or isolated mini-grids; propose effective and efficient tariffs in the context of mini-grid solutions with least-cost technology approaches; and establish rules to ensure investment certainty in cases when the main grid reaches the mini-grid.

Beyond the regulatory need and governance, this report briefly touches on a scenario for further Indonesian electricity sector transformation. This transformation would also have consequences for the roles and impacts of the regulatory body. In a scenario with further sector transformation, we suggest the government to unbundle PLN into generation and transmission. The unbundling form should be structural, i.e., at least two separate companies should be either owning generation or transmission infrastructure (ownership unbundling). This form of unbundling will require the least degree of regulatory oversight compared to its alternatives (e.g., unbundling of accounts). We suggest the government establish an ISO model that creates a central dispatch authority to make it more comparable to the current structure in Indonesia.

We do not suggest that the government divide Indonesia into several electricity jurisdictions; i.e., the structures, institutions, frameworks, and regulatory processes should be alike in all parts of the country. In case current structures prohibit the implementation of one single approach for the entire country at the same time, we suggest to identify reasons for requiring temporary separation, as well as clearly elaborate on measures to overcome the separation within a defined timeline. Implementation of these measures should be made binding to the institution(s) responsible for their implementation and progress made against an established timeline needs to be monitored and enforced.

Introduction

The establishment of a regulatory body for Indonesia's electricity sector has been considered for some years, and the establishment of this body has also been attempted in the past. Our analysis found evidence for a positive contribution of an Indonesian electricity regulatory body in various areas, one of which is the Special Task Force for Upstream Oil and Gas Business Activities (SKK Migas) that works across regulatory making, procurement, and monitoring of upstream business activities in the oil and gas sector. Whereas existing regulatory bodies in various sectors profess enhanced effectivity, the implementation and operation of a regulatory body requires to be implemented in the context of the Indonesian Constitution and related judicial rulings issued by the Constitutional Court of Indonesia (MK) especially with respect to the relevant sector.

Indonesian laws on electricity have been reviewed several times by MK and in most cases, the concerns are similar; how to define the proper limit of state control in the electricity sector given the provision of Article 33 of the 1945 Indonesian Constitution. Indeed, a 2002 version of the proposed electricity law was fully revoked by MK as the court determined that the law failed to meet the minimum standard of state control. In this context, MK introduced five principles of state control through which the government can employ its tools of power: policy, actions, regulation, management, and supervision. These constitutional requirements to maintain state control over the Indonesian electricity sector ultimately affect the structures in which a regulatory body can operate its staffing and tasks in the electricity industry including its decision-making competence.

This report describes why a regulatory body is generally used in the context of electricity sector governance, how regulatory bodies can be governed to ensure high-quality decisions, and the functions a regulatory body can have, as stipulated in Section 1. The report further elaborates on the key legal environment for the Indonesian electricity system, including the ultimate question on whether a regulatory body would be deemed unconstitutional as stipulated in Section 2. Section 3 describes a list of tasks the Indonesian electricity regulatory body is to initially perform to optimize the sector's performance within the existing market structures. Section 4 provides a first assessment on how to successfully establish an Indonesian electricity regulatory body considering legal circumstances, roles and responsibilities of other stakeholders, and expertise required. Section 5 closes with an outlook on additional regulatory functions associated to a possible new market structure, structured with a stronger degree of unbundling, including the full separation of certain functions away from the State Electricity Company of Indonesia (PLN). Throughout all sections, cases from other jurisdictions are used to strengthen a specific aspect or recommendation.

Why a Regulatory Body Matters

There are two main principles that justify regulatory oversight in electricity systems. First, electricity is an essential service required by the public, businesses, and individuals. Second, because of the technical nature of the electricity system, a single network service provider is often able to serve the overall demand at a lower total cost than any combination of network entities. As competition and companies are poised to fail within integrated structures to a degree that resembles a natural monopoly, eventually all firms but one will exit the market. The surviving utility integrates network and other services and will be able to exert its market power as it remains uncontested in the market. Therefore, economic regulation applied to the noncompetitive segment of the electricity sector is the government's response to keep the lights on and avoid services being supplied by a sole provider.

The main reason for the introduction of regulatory bodies is that those authorities present a neutral decision maker, equipped with powers to implement policies and policy objectives issued by government. Regulatory bodies support the delivery of investment and protect customers. Decisions made by regulatory bodies commonly seek to establish and maintain a balance between policy targets, investors, and other stakeholders.

Historically, electricity sector regulatory bodies have been established to address the economic disparity between customers and monopoly electricity service providers via oversight. With changing technologies and political circumstances, regulatory bodies often evolve to play a significant role in modernizing the electricity system through supporting regional trade, renewable energy technologies, and smart grid technology deployment.

High-performing regulatory bodies are an important institutional player in electricity markets as they can guide electricity sector decision-making while guaranteeing "fair" regulations to all sector stakeholders. To that end, high-quality regulatory decisions are critical. Among others, regulators often set tariffs, decide investment plans, approve contracts, and monitor and enforce behavior. How the electricity regulatory body is established, directed, controlled, resourced, and held accountable are all factors that influence the quality of the organization's decision-making. These factors define the nature of the relationships between the regulatory body, the political decision makers, the regulated entities, and the electricity consumers. The management of these factors directly influences the level of trust in the regulatory authority and ultimately the sector's overall performance.

As "referee" to the sector, a regulatory body can avoid the emergence of conflict of interest resulting from policy formulation and implementation being centralized in one institution. Regulators have the advantage to provide continuous attention to any required area of concern in the electricity sector. A dedicated long-term approach, combined with an adequate resource base and staffing policy, encourages the attraction, development, and retention of the required sector expertise. A high-quality regulatory body continuously engages in the electricity sector, which allows for a continuous and credible adjustment of sector direction in small steps.

Governments across the globe have implemented electricity regulatory bodies to implement sector policies and optimize sectoral behavior. Among Organisation for Economic Co-operation and Development (OECD) economies, only Japan and the Republic of Korea have not introduced an electricity regulatory body, while several countries such as Canada, Germany, and the United States have multiple electricity regulatory bodies based on state-level jurisdictional boundaries. Beyond the OECD, very few countries have chosen not to implement regulatory bodies, including Tajikistan, Turkmenistan, and Uzbekistan (Central Asia); Suriname and Venezuela (Latin America); Kuwait, Lebanon, and Qatar (Middle East); Libya (Northern Africa); and Botswana, Democratic Republic of Congo, Djibouti, and Eritrea (sub-Saharan Africa). Alongside Brunei Darussalam and the Lao People's Democratic Republic, Indonesia is left behind as one of the few countries without a dedicated electricity regulatory body in Southeast Asia.

Ensuring High-Quality Regulatory Decisions

High-quality regulatory decisions, i.e., decisions which are evidence-based, acceptable and, provide net benefits on the organization's objectives, result from an environment of regulatory governance, mechanisms, and structures. According to OECD (OECD, 2014) providing such an environment ultimately requires recognizing the relevance of seven areas:

1. *Role clarity,* which supports an effective regulatory body through clear objectives and functions as well as a means to coordinate with all required stakeholders to achieve the desired regulatory outcomes.

2. *Trust and prevention of undue influence,* which can be enabled through the integrity of regulatory decisions.

3. *Decision-making structure and governing body within the regulatory body,* which enables regulatory bodies to maintain their effective functioning, preserve decision-making integrity, and deliver on mandated objectives.

4. *Accountability and transparency,* which regulated entities must uphold to the public in order to maintain the proper application of public authority and use of resources, mirroring expectations from ministers and the legislature.

5. *Engagement,* which regulatory bodies use to prepare, take, and communicate decisions with stakeholders without being subject to conflicts of interest.

6. *Funding,* which allows regulatory operations and decision-making without undue influence or distortions, and should be sufficient in amount and reliable in its source.

7. *Performance evaluation,* which allows the regulatory body to receive feedback on the impacts of their decisions, continuously make changes in line with objectives, demonstrate the effectiveness to whom it is accountable, and build confidence in the regulatory system.

These areas summarized here constitute the knowledge base for assessing key considerations to introduce a regulatory body into the Indonesian electricity sector as described in Section 3.

Regulatory Functions in the Electricity Sector

The scope of the main regulatory functions varies to reflect each country-specific context. The following provides an overview of possible regulatory functions as observed globally.

Table 1:   Possible Regulatory Functions Overview

Licensing	Licensing aims to enable the licensee to provide its specific services in the sector. Common licenses in the electricity sector include transmission, distribution, interconnectors, generation, and the supply of electricity to premises. Licensing commonly follows a clearly defined process to be completed prior to the start of services and often involves a fee. Examples of commonly applied criteria when deciding whether to grant a license include checks on integrity of the application; insolvency history; financial viability (e.g., charging arrangements, credit rating, indebtedness); compliance with sector rules such as provisions for unbundling, customer protection, or industry codes; security, availability, and quality of service; operation and maintenance provisions; and supply area coverage.
Economic regulation	Economic regulation depends on the overall structure of the electricity market, which can cover network and generation services or only network services (the latter when the provision of and demand for generation services are provided within fully competitive market structures). Economic regulation comprises the determination of regulated entities' revenue requirements and the approval of service rates for consumers. Where applied, economic regulation is often linked to regulated infrastructure investment planning and siting processes.
Contract regulation	Contract regulation is applied at the intersection between customers and generation service providers, with detailed regulatory requirements differing from the underlying market structure. In markets with fully competitive structures, contract regulation often encompasses monitoring and analysis of price and volume offers. Under these conditions, further contract details (e.g., transmission access rules, cost allocation for network services, technical service quality standards) can often be influenced by a diverse set of market rules governed by various bodies. In markets with less competitive structures, contract regulation can include template standardization (or less rigid forms of regulatory intervention) and price and volume setting for power sales.
Standards for electric services	Standards for electric services are often adopted from industry standards for voltage, frequency, and other technical requirements such as environmental impacts. Regulatory decisions often also include the establishment of processes by which customers may be disconnected for nonpayment and service quality indexes to measure the quality of utility service (e.g., frequency and duration of outages, the speed with which companies respond to telephone inquiries, and the speed with which they respond to unsafe conditions).
Investment planning regulations	Investment planning regulations offer coverage similar to economic regulation (generation and networks or networks only). Regulatory decisions for infrastructure planning can include the determination and/or approval of electricity system needs and the determination and/or approval of measures to be implemented, including technology choices at specific sizes, locations, and time. Investment planning often follows clearly defined processes and can inform economic regulation and infrastructure siting.
Infrastructure siting	Infrastructure siting often builds upon the results of investment planning. Siting identifies strategic and specific socioenvironmental impacts, and the regulatory body can ensure the infrastructure proponent has considered opinions and information brought by all parties involved. Additionally, siting decisions often conclude with the determination of specific technologies and measures to be used, and the decision of where to locate the infrastructure. Comparable to investment planning, siting often is guided by clearly defined rules.
Prudence review	Prudence review can be applied following the completion of the asset development to determine if the infrastructure was constructed or implemented as proposed, is in accordance with sound management practices, and has been built at a reasonable cost and with care. This review may compare utility performance to a previously reviewed set of goals, or it may be prepared on an ad hoc basis for a specific project.
Energy efficiency	Energy efficiency is sometimes required based on standards for buildings, appliances, and other equipment. Regulatory decision-making often provides a mechanism to recover the utilities' investments.
Financing regulations	Financing regulations are sometimes applied. These grant regulatory permissions to refinance utility assets. This leads to reasonable security terms and keeps debt levels acceptable, which supports access to capital markets.

Source: Authors.

Legal Circumstances for an Electricity Regulatory Body in Indonesia

When considering the introduction of a regulatory body in the Indonesian electricity sector, the legal environment sets relevant boundaries. The constitutional requirement to maintain state control over the Indonesian electricity sector ultimately affects the structures in which a regulatory body can operate its staffing and its decision-making competence.

The Legal Conditions Surrounding the Regulatory Body

The current regulatory framework on electricity in Indonesia is provided in the 2009 Electricity Law and its implementing regulations: Government Regulation No. 14 of 2012 (as amended by Government Regulation No. 23 of 2014) on Electricity Business Provision (GR 14/2012), Government Regulation No. 42 of 2012 on Cross-Border Sale and Purchases (GR 42/2012), Government Regulation No. 62 of 2012 on Electricity Support Business (GR 62/2012), and other implementing regulations issued by MEMR, Ministry of Industry, MOF, Ministry of Environment and Forestry, and other ministries with relevant responsibilities relating to the electricity sector. We set out a list of regulations related to electricity in Indonesia in Appendix 6 and the relevant stakeholders in the electricity sector in Appendix 2.

Three main versions of electricity laws have shaped the Indonesian electricity sector; one in 1985, one in 2002 replacing the 1985 law (which was later deemed unconstitutional), and finally, the latest one issued in 2009.

The highlight of Law No. 15 of 1985 on Electricity (1985 Electricity Law) was the centralization of the Indonesian electricity sector through PLN as the sole state-owned electricity company that, until now, holds the exclusive power over the transmission, distribution, and sale of electricity.[1] We set out a further explanation of the 1985 Electricity Law in Appendix 3.

In 2002, the government reformed the electricity business in Indonesia through the enactment of Law No. 20 of 2002 on Electricity (2002 Electricity Law). In connection with the scope of business for the electricity sector, the 2002 Electricity Law regulated two major types of business: electricity supply business and electricity support services. Under the 2002 Electricity Law, the electricity business was divided into competitive and noncompetitive areas. The competitive area allowing for private participation in the generation and retail areas of the electricity value chain.[2] We set out a further explanation of the distinction between competitive and noncompetitive areas in Appendix 3. The 2002 Electricity Law also introduced the Electricity Market Supervisory Agency (BPPTL) that had the authority and responsibility to make independent decisions to carry out the regulation and supervision of electricity supply only in areas where competition applies, along with the duties of (i) implementing rules that would encourage the creation of a competitive market in the generation and retail

---

[1]   Government of Indonesia. 1985. *Electricity Law (Article 7)*. Jakarta.
[2]   Government of Indonesia. 2002. *Electricity Law (Article 6(2) and Article 9(1))*. Jakarta.

Figure 1: Current Institutional Structure of the Electricity Sector of Indonesia

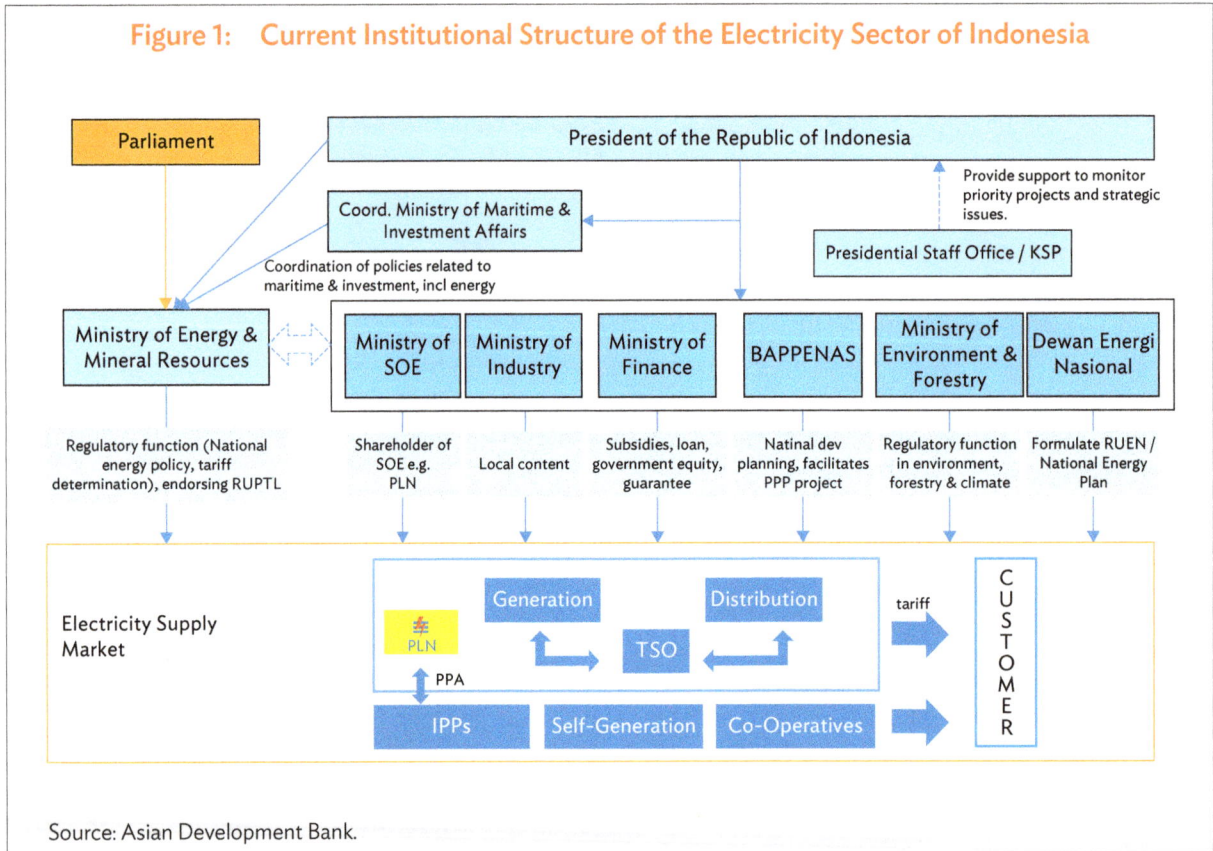

Source: Asian Development Bank.

Figure 2: Milestone of Regulatory Framework on Electricity in Indonesia

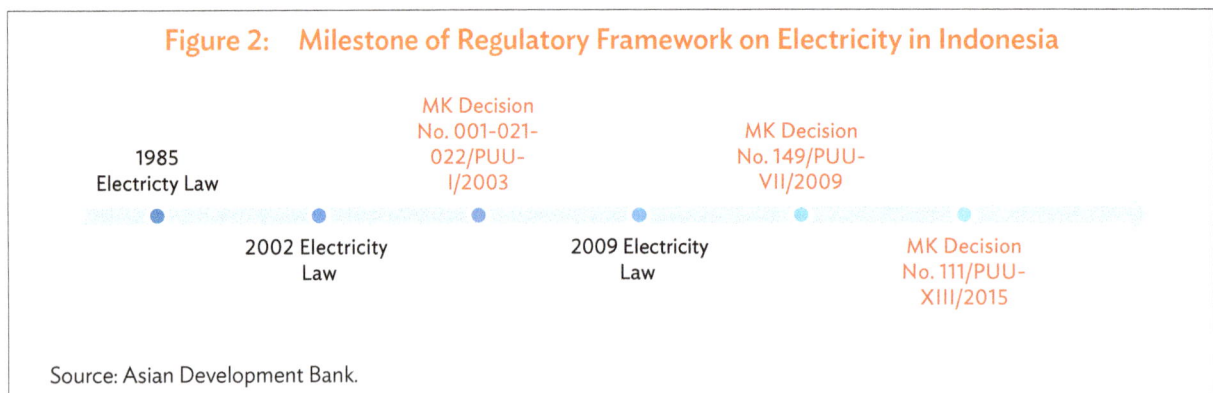

Source: Asian Development Bank.

sale of electricity and (ii) make arrangements in the field of transmission and distribution, including arrangements for the transition from the monopoly market to a competitive market. Under Government Regulation No. 53 of 2003 on BPPTL (GR 53/2003), BPPTL was an independent body authorized to make decisions without being influenced by other parts of the government.[3] It was authorized to (i) elaborate and apply the government's general policies in regulating electricity supply businesses; (ii) prevent unfair business competition; (iii) regulate the selling price of electricity in the electricity sales business,[4] the cost of providing facilities to maintain the quality and reliability of the electric power system, and the price of transmission rents and the rental price of

---

3   Government of Indonesia. 2003. *Government Regulation No. 53 (Article 2)*. Jakarta.
4   Footnote 2, Article 1(9)

electricity distribution; (iv) supervise the selling price of electricity for specific sectors of the electricity generation and electricity sales agents (ESAs) that were subject to competition.; (v) regulate and supervise the business of electricity market managers and electric power system managers; (vi) determine the area of distribution and business of electric power sales; (vii) issue the electricity supply business permit (IUPTL) for each type of electricity supply business; and (viii) apply administrative sanctions to holders of IUPTL for violations of the provisions of laws and permits.[5]

The MEMR had the authority to submit a list of prospective members for BPPTL to be approved by the President after MEMR obtained approval from the House of Representatives (DPR). BPPTL was required to submit regular reports to the President. Also, BPPTL had an obligation to submit a work plan and budget that later will be stipulated by the minister of Finance after obtaining MEMR's approval for its work plan and budget.[6]

Under Article 8 (2) of the 2002 Electricity Law, there were seven types of businesses under the definition of being an electricity supply business: (i) electricity generation that produces electricity; (ii) electricity transmission that distributes electricity from a source of generation to a distribution system or to consumers, or distribution of electricity between systems; (iii) electric power distribution that distributes electricity from the transmission system or from the generation system to consumers; (iv) electricity sales business that sells electricity to customers who are connected to low-voltage grid; (v) an ESA that sells electricity to customers connected to high and middle voltage grid; (vi) electricity market manager that has the function of meeting supply and demand of electricity, confirming electricity tariff, and settling transactions and disputes between market players; and (vii) electricity system manager that has the function of controlling and coordinating the power system, dispatching operation to power generators, and securing electricity supply.

A business entity that conducted any type of an electricity supply business must hold an IUPTL in accordance with the type of electricity supply business such business entity conducts. An IUPTL will only be given after the relevant business entity has fulfilled the administrative and technical requirements.

Furthermore, the 2002 Electricity Law differentiated the sale and purchase mechanism between ESAs that conduct the sale and purchase of electricity for customers that are connected to high and middle-grid voltage networks, and electricity sales businesses that conduct sale and purchase of electricity for customers that are connected to low-grid voltage. Below is the diagram on the sale and purchase mechanism under the 2002 Electricity Law.

In December 2004, MK ruled the 2002 Electricity Law to be entirely unconstitutional on the basis that it contravened Article 33 of the Indonesian Constitution through Decision 001. According to Decision 001, electricity is a strategic commodity and its generation and distribution should remain under the exclusive control of the government. Consequently, MK re-enacted the previous 1985 Electricity Law. We set out the summary of the MK Decision 001 in Appendix 3.

It is worth noting that Decision 001 argued that the 2002 Electricity Law was annulled due to the existence of Article 16, Article 17 paragraph (3), and Article 68 of the 2002 Electricity Law on unbundling of electricity business and introducing competition; therefore the core provisions of the 2002 Electricity Law were not in line with the Indonesian Constitution. As such, the constitutionality of the BPPTL establishment was not discussed in Decision 001 even though the elucidation of the 2002 Electricity Law stated that the existence of BPPTL would

---

[5]   Footnote 3, Article 4
[6]   Footnote 3, Article 17.

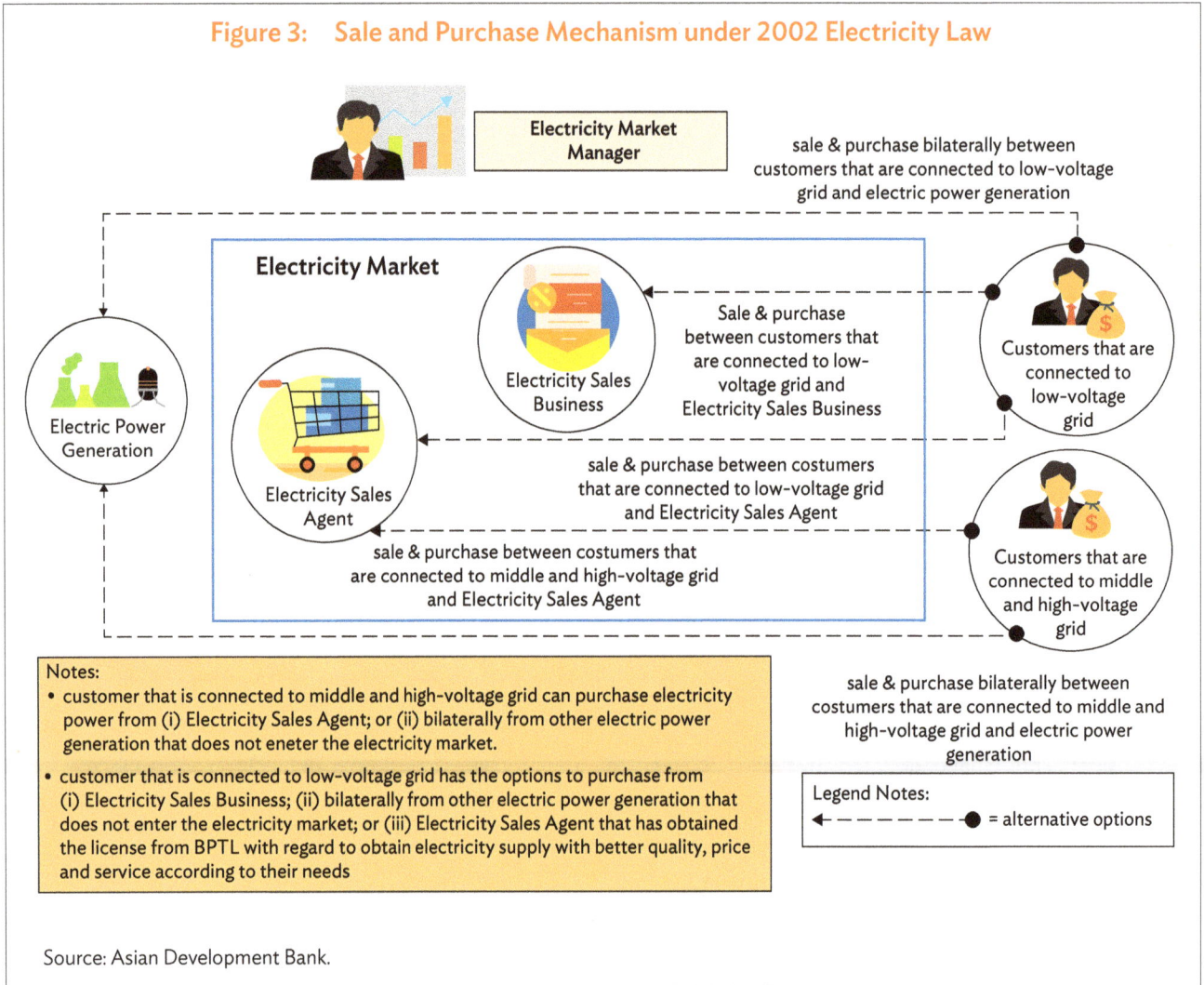

Figure 3:   Sale and Purchase Mechanism under 2002 Electricity Law

Electricity Market Manager

sale & purchase bilaterally between customers that are connected to low-voltage grid and electric power generation

Electricity Market

Electricity Sales Business

Electric Power Generation

Sale & purchase between customers that are connected to low-voltage grid and Electricity Sales Business

Customers that are connected to low-voltage grid

Electricity Sales Agent

sale & purchase between costumers that are connected to low-voltage grid and Electricity Sales Agent

sale & purchase between costumers that are connected to middle and high-voltage grid and Electricity Sales Agent

Customers that are connected to middle and high-voltage grid

sale & purchase bilaterally between costumers that are connected to middle and high-voltage grid and electric power generation

Notes:
• customer that is connected to middle and high-voltage grid can purchase electricity power from (i) Electricity Sales Agent; or (ii) bilaterally from other electric power generation that does not eneter the electricity market.
• customer that is connected to low-voltage grid has the options to purchase from (i) Electricity Sales Business; (ii) bilaterally from other electric power generation that does not enter the electricity market; or (iii) Electricity Sales Agent that has obtained the license from BPTL with regard to obtain electricity supply with better quality, price and service according to their needs

Legend Notes:
◄ — — — — — ● = alternative options

Source: Asian Development Bank.

reduce the role of the government in stipulating electricity business regulations (though not necessarily the authority of the government as a policy maker).

In 2009, the government issued the 2009 Electricity Law to strengthen the regulatory framework and provide a greater role for regional governments in terms of licensing and determining electricity tariffs. The 2009 Electricity Law replaced the 1985 Electricity Law and, taking into account Decision 001, removed the concept of competition and unbundling system in the electricity sector.

Article 3 of the 2009 Electricity Law stipulates that electricity is one of the most important and strategic production branches; therefore, the electricity supply should be controlled by the state while the operation is carried out by the government and regional governments based on the existing regional autonomy principle. This was designated to ensure that the implementation maximizes the welfare and prosperity of the people. The law is also in place to ensure business implementation of electricity supply is open for state-owned enterprises (SOEs), region-owned enterprises, private business entities, cooperatives, and nongovernment organizations.

The scope of business under the 2009 Electricity Law covers electricity supply businesses (either for public use or own use). Under Article 10 of the law, there are 4 types of businesses under the definition of an electricity supply business for public use: (i) electricity generation, (ii) electricity transmission, (iii) electricity distribution, and (iv) sales of electricity.

Electricity supply business that provides electricity for public interest shall be carried out by one business entity in a business area.[7] Limitation of business area applies to the electricity supply businesses for public purposes which only cover electricity distribution and/or sale of electricity.[8] The business entities operating the electricity supply for public interests include SOEs (prioritized), region-owned enterprises, private business entities, cooperatives, and nongovernment organizations.[9] While this seems to promote competition among multiple entities, in practice, PLN's business area covers the entire area of Indonesia other than those areas that have been specifically granted to an entity as may be approved by the MEMR. These rules are mandated under Article 11 of the 2009 Electricity Law that the government will give priority to an SOE operating in the electricity supply sector (i.e., PLN) in the implementation of electricity supply for public purposes in Indonesia.[10]

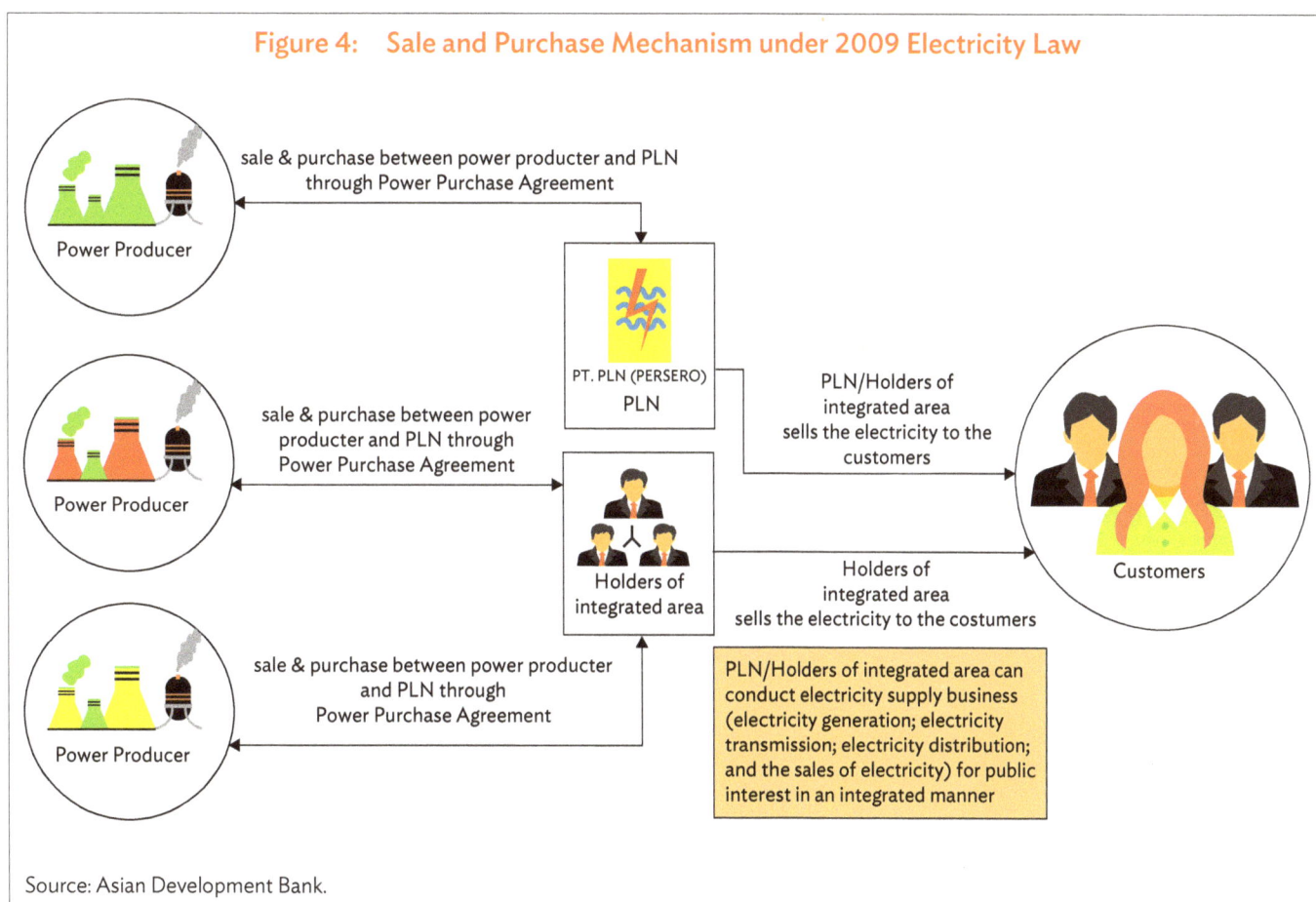

Figure 4:   Sale and Purchase Mechanism under 2009 Electricity Law

Source: Asian Development Bank.

---

[7]   Government of Indonesia. 2009. *Electricity Law (Article 10 (3))*. Jakarta.
[8]   Footnote 7, Article 10 (4).
[9]   Footnote 7, (Article 11).
[10] Footnote 7.

Based on Article 33 of the 2009 Electricity Law, the selling prices of electrical power and lease of electrical power networks must be stipulated based on the principles of fair competition. The holders of IUPTLs must first get approval from the government or regional governments before applying the selling prices of electrical power and lease of electrical power networks. Furthermore, based on Article 34 of the 2009 Electricity Law, the government shall stipulate the electric power tariffs for customers with the approval of the DPR, and the regional governments shall stipulate the electrical power tariffs for customers with the approval of the Regional House of Representatives.

In 2009 through MK Decision No. 149/PUU-VII/2009 (Decision 149), the current 2009 Electricity Law was challenged by the PLN Labor Union on the basis that the 2009 Electricity Law opens up private participation in power supply and distribution which ended PLN's monopoly.[11] The idea was to challenge the unbundling concept contained in the 2009 Electricity Law. The PLN Labor Union also argued that Article 10 of the 2009 Electricity Law includes the phrase "may be conducted in an integrated manner" which implies that it may or may not be integrated or it may be unbundled, which violates Article 33 of the Indonesian Constitution.[12] The full text of Article 10 of the 2009 Electricity Law states that "public power supply business (power generation, power transmission, power distribution, and/or power sales) may be conducted in an integrated manner." A summary of MK Decision 149 is provided in Appendix 3.

On 14 December 2016, MK issued its MK Decision No. 111/PUU-XIII/2015 (Decision 111) which reconsidered the constitutionality of certain provisions of the 2009 Electricity Law that deal with Indonesia's electricity regulatory framework, particularly the constitutionality of private sector involvement in the provision of electricity to the Indonesian public. While the decision itself did not directly revoke any provision of the 2009 Electricity Law as it applied the concept of "conditionally unconstitutional" against the reviewed provisions, it created yet another vague standard in reading and implementing the 2009 Electricity Law. We set out the summary of Decision 111 in Appendix 3.

A Regulatory Body Does Not Reduce State Control

When Indonesian electricity laws have been reviewed by MK in the past, the nature and limit of state control in the electricity business has been a recurring focus of attention. This focus is evident as the electricity business falls under the term "sectors of production which are important for the country and affect the life of the people."

Decision 001 (as also quoted in Decision 149 and Decision 111) states that the concept of state control in the Indonesian Constitution has a broader definition than the concept of private ownership under civil law. MK stated that if the definition of state control is only interpreted to mean private ownership under the civil law concept, it will not satisfy the purpose of "achieving the greatest prosperity of the people" and the mandate to "advance public welfare" and "provide social justice for all the people of Indonesia." In fact, for MK, the definition of state control also cannot be simply limited to the government's authority to regulate. According to MK, an accurate description of state control must cover the government's mandate in performing the following authorities:

1. *Policy function.* The government's power to make policies, including detailed planning in performing government administration activities and directing private parties in running their business activities. In planning, the government must follow various processes and/or stages involving a multitude of stakeholders in accordance with applicable laws.

---

[11] Alfian. 2010. PLN Labor Union to Challenge New Law on Electricity. *The Jakarta Post.* 20 January. http://www.thejakartapost.com/news/2010/01/20/pln-labor-union-challenge-new-law-electricity.html

[12] Footnote 11.

2. *Action function*. The government's authority to issue and revoke permits, licenses, and concessions to third parties.

3. *Regulation function*. The government's authority (in collaboration with the DPR as lawmakers) to enact laws in the forms of statutes, government regulations, and other forms of regulation and decrees.

4. *Management function*. The government's authority to manage the vast resources of Indonesia for the greatest prosperity of the people through shareholding mechanisms, direct investment, and/or direct control in the management of SOEs or state-owned legal entities.

5. *Supervision function*. The government's authority to supervise the implementation of state control of production branches that are important to and/or affect the livelihood of the people to ensure these production branches are truly and properly used for the greatest prosperity of the people.

Based on MK Decision No. 36/PUU-X/2012 on Judicial Review of Law No. 22 of 2001 on Oil and Gas (the Oil and Gas Law) (Decision 36), MK introduced another perspective in defining state control and focusing on the practice by offering three possible interpretations:

1. *Strong involvement*. The government directly runs and operates all essential sectors and natural resources management (minimizing private actor's involvement, if not making it obsolete).

2. *Medium involvement*. The government sets the relevant policies for the relevant sector by establishing a detailed plan to be followed by industry players and implements its licensing power by granting, amending, and/or revoking the licenses and concessions to private parties.

3. *Weak involvement*. The government focuses its efforts only on issuing regulation and supervising the activities of private parties. The state is not directly involved in operating the business nor does it exercise any licensing power.

Given the vague boundaries set out under the Indonesian Constitution and MK decisions as mentioned above, it is not clear whether the above five principles of state control must always be maintained at all times or whether there could be differing degrees of implementation. It is unclear where the government has the freedom to determine its own level of involvement in the management of sectors and natural resources with strategic importance to Indonesia.

Based on the above conceptual analysis, the establishment of an Indonesian electricity regulatory body does not necessarily mean that it would undermine the government's power to exercise its "state control." Indeed, tracing back to Decision 001, MK has never explicitly rejected an electricity regulatory body as a possible institution for Indonesia. However, certain guidelines must still be followed to minimize the risk of Indonesian judicial authorities declaring that a regulatory body is unconstitutional. Do note that MK's judicial review authority is solely limited to laws or statutes. Any judicial review of regulations below laws or statutes will be subject to the authority of the Supreme Court of Indonesia (MA) and in practice, MA does not always follow the opinions of MK.

Returning to the guidelines, a good example where a regulatory body was deemed unconstitutional, under the pretext of lessening state control, was the Oil and Gas Upstream Business Activities Operational Agency (BP Migas). Through Decision 36, MK declared certain provisions of Oil and Gas Law on BP Migas to be unconstitutional since, according to MK, BP Migas significantly reduced the government's ability to exercise its management and action functions, such as, by limiting the government's licensing power and forcing the government to enter into private contract with private parties (instead of exercising such licensing power), and also by limiting the government to manage the relevant natural resources through SOEs.

One way that might help in avoiding the above issue is to have the new regulator as part of MEMR, which means that such a body will directly report to and be under the supervision of MEMR. There is no doubt that MEMR cannot be separated from the government and that MEMR, given its role, should be considered as a perfect example of how the government exercises its state control power. Also, as will be further discussed below, establishing a new department in the MEMR would not be too complicated in terms of choosing the level of implementing regulations as the basis of establishing such a body. Yet, we will also need to consider whether having the body as a new division in the MEMR would render the body to be ineffective or even worse, not independent.

In the context of state control, it is relevant to determine the limit of government's authority in controlling and managing the electricity sector as embodied in Article 5 of the 2009 Electricity Law which stipulates, among others

"The authority of the Government in electricity sector includes:

(a) *Determination of national policies in electricity sector;*

(b) *Determination of laws and regulations in electricity sector; ..."*

The above provisions are broad in nature, which create unclear boundaries that are difficult to navigate, particularly on the following crucial matters: (i) whether the 2009 Electricity Law allows the establishment of an independent regulatory body that may or may not be detached from the government; and (ii) whether the government authorities under Article 5 of the 2009 Electricity Law could and/or should be partially or entirely delegated to the regulatory body, as part of national policy or laws and regulations.

First, though the 2009 Electricity Law does not explicitly mention the existence of an independent regulatory body in the electricity sector (unlike the 2002 Electricity Law), Article 5 of the 2009 Electricity Law also does not specifically restrict the authority of the government to establish such body. As highlighted by Jimly Asshiddiqie, a prominent legal scholar and also the former chief justice of MK, the state's policy-making function is related to the state's ability to build a grand plan for achieving certain objectives, such as the maintenance of security and order (Asshiddiqie: 2006, 34). Due to the broadly defined function, there is room to argue that the establishment of a regulatory body is a part of government's grand plan of policies in the electricity sector.

Moreover, according to Asshidiqqie, the establishment of an independent regulatory body is usually motivated by the implementation of how the existing government can no longer fulfill the need of the public interest efficiently and effectively (Asshiddiqie: 2006, 27).

Furthermore, since a state body or agency can only be established by laws and/or regulations, it may also be argued that the establishment of a regulatory body is a part of the government's exercise of its own authority under Article 5 paragraph (1) (b) of the 2009 Electricity Law, which includes the determination of laws and regulations in the electricity sector.

Second, based on our interviews with several stakeholders in the electricity sector, most of them believe that the MEMR has not sufficiently taken an active role in supervising and developing the electricity business sector. They suspect that this was due to MEMR's lack of technical experts in the electricity business activities. If their assessment is accurate, the establishment of a regulatory body might enhance the capabilities of MEMR in performing its regulatory and supervisory power, and this would be aligned with MK's concept of five key principles of state control.

Key Tasks for an Indonesian Electricity Regulatory Body

Due to the growing demand for electricity, the Indonesian electricity sector needs to attract significant investments in the years to come. Based on the 2019 RUPTL, the expected average electricity demand growth in the next 10 years in Indonesia is 6.42%. To accommodate the growing demand, PLN foresees the need to install around 56 gigawatts of additional power generation capacity through 2028. The associated investment needs are bigger than current levels of investment from PLN, the subnational level, and the private sector combined. Furthermore, the existing infrastructure is used inefficiently, incurring unnecessary costs to PLN (and other service providers).

The World Bank Infrastructure Sector Assessment Program in its 2018 report (World Bank, 2018) highlights a resulting infrastructure gap in the electricity sector (and other sectors) and provides recommendations on how the Government of Indonesia could close this gap in the future. Among others, the report recommends the establishment of a strong regulatory body in the electricity sector.

This section of the report details such a regulatory body for the Indonesian electricity sector, discussing the possible regulatory functions needed in order to tackle specific issues identified as part of Asian Development Bank's own sector assessment conducted in the first half of 2019.

The guiding principle of our assessment is to promote a regulatory body which contributes to the optimization of the current Indonesian electricity market structure. This assessment does not seek to promote regulatory functions or market structures that are not in line with the Indonesian constitution.

The Asian Development Bank assessment revealed possible themes in the electricity sector where a regulatory body can contribute with a positive outcome: infrastructure planning, infrastructure procurement, and efficient cost recovery and allocation.

Evidence from other jurisdictions suggest that regulatory bodies can positively influence decisions made as part of the abovementioned themes. As such, if appropriately set up and used, an Indonesian electricity regulatory body is likely to contribute to an environment which attracts timely and efficient investment and promotes the efficient provision and use of electricity services. According to opinions expressed by stakeholders in the Indonesian electricity sector, establishing a regulatory body for electricity could lead to enhanced supervision and development of the sector.

Infrastructure Planning

The Indonesian electricity sector centers on PLN as the main supplier of electricity. PLN owns and operates around 60% of the total installed electricity generation capacity (PWC, 2018). PLN also functions as a single buyer for electricity generated by independent power producers (IPP). IPPs own and operate around 40% of total installed capacity, selling all electricity directly to PLN at prices established through power purchase agreements (PPAs).

Infrastructure planning, in the context of the Indonesian electricity system, is commonly applied and used within market structures similar to the Indonesian single buyer model. Infrastructure planning can comprise generation and transmission assets, with the aim to identify

1. the right technology mix to ensure reliable and affordable supply with electricity, while ensuring that relevant public policy targets are met;

2. the need for investment in terms of location, size, and timing;

3. the way forward in terms of procuring associated assets; and

4. progress made in the asset delivery against commissioning targets.

Infrastructure plans are commonly used as a direct linkage between public policy objectives and specific investment to advance the electricity sector. Infrastructure plans are distinct from government plans, which are used to inform or develop policy direction and targets as well as to develop the right set of policies and measures. The distinction between the plans (government plans vs. investment plans) is further relevant as the planning principles and roles of stakeholders differ—the development of government plans has only indirect implications on infrastructure and is often used by the government as a strategic tool. Often, government plans cover a longer period compared to infrastructure plans. However, only infrastructure plans (usually) involve a diverse set of stakeholders. The following therefore focuses on infrastructure planning.

Government, investors, consumers, and other stakeholders all look at infrastructure plans with different considerations in mind. Governments are predominantly concerned about congruency of the plan's outcomes and established policy targets (e.g., Will the planned and developed assets ensure supply of electricity at a targeted reliability level? Does the plan deliver on an established share of renewables in the electricity system?) as well as wider acceptance of and ability to implement the plan (on time). Investors look at infrastructure plans with a view to assess the implications on the existing assets they hold, as well as on concrete future business opportunities, including associated risks (e.g., technology risks, delivery risks, financial risks) and risk mitigation requirements (e.g., through engineering, procurement, and construction or power sales contracting). Consumers and other stakeholders (e.g., environmental groups) are mostly concerned about quality of supply at least cost when considering all technology alternatives, and also about the congruency of the plan's outcomes with societal norms and expectations (e.g., Will the plan deliver local jobs? Does the plan create long-term liabilities to society?). A subset of consumers will also expect to be able to have an influence on aspects related to the use of land and also discuss alternative options in preparation for infrastructure siting.

Irrespective of stakeholders' interest in the plan, its relevance is essential to all participants. Only a program that is perceived to be relevant by all stakeholders has the potential to be fully accepted and, consequently, be implemented in time.

In order to legitimize the relevance of a plan, it should be established in accordance with specific planning elements, including a legal foundation, and managed by a planning entity with planning objectives. The plan should feature stakeholder engagement, transparency, and incorporate investment selection methodologies (see for example International Renewable Energy Agency, 2018 for a more comprehensive discussion on planning elements). The requirement to develop and use a plan is often prescribed through sector law. This legal foundation can provide general certainty about fundamentals such as the roles of different stakeholders as well as the process to develop a plan and deliver on its results.

The Indonesian legal environment requires the development of two plans, which are the foundation for a third plan. The National Electricity Master Plan (RUKN) and the Regional Electricity Plan (RUKD) are enshrined in the 2009 Electricity Law. The 2009 Electricity Law requires that Indonesia must have a RUKN developed by MEMR and multiple RUKDs developed by regional governments. RUKN is basically a 20-year projection of electricity demand and supply that describes the related investment and funding policy and the utilization plan for new and renewable energy resources. RUKN is developed based on the National Energy Policy, which is currently stipulated under GR 79/2014. Furthermore, under MEMR 24/2015, RUKN is drafted by MEMR on behalf of the government along with several consultation sessions with DPR. RUKN is subject to review once every 3 years, at the very least. Under the 2009 Electricity Law, all RUKD must be prepared based on the applicable RUKN.

The Electricity Supply Business Plan (RUPTL) complements the RUKN and RUKD. The RUPTL constitutes a 10-year electricity development plan in the business area(s), which is based on the RUKN and RUKD. The RUPTL results in projects that are planned to be developed by PLN and IPPs. The RUPTL is reviewed annually. The procurement route for IPPs to build power plants is also based on the RUPTL. The RUPTL is meant to be the guiding document for all investors in the Indonesian power sector, and, as such, is the focus of our assessment.

Several analytical assessments suggest shortcomings with the process for and results of the current investment plan, the RUPTL.

There seems to be a general lack of transparency leading to the formulation of the RUPTL, including the data used, assumptions made, and tools applied in the formulation of the plan. There is no stakeholder inclusion at any stage of the development of the RUPTL, and only the final outcome is currently made available. The most recent RUPTL seems to be misaligned with the RUKN. For example, for 2028, the draft RUKN (2018–2037) projects an electricity demand of close to 700 terawatt-hours, while for the same year, the RUPTL (2018–2027) projects a demand of around 500 terawatt-hours. Also, for 2025, MEMR projects in the RUKN (2015–2034) have an energy mix of less than 25% oil and over 30% of coal. For the same year, the RUPTL (2018–2027) projects an energy mix using 0.4% oil and 54.4% coal for electricity production (see RUKN 2015 and RUPTL 2018). Furthermore, it is unclear which reliability target is incorporated into the plan and how this target is going to be met. A lack of transparency in the RUPTL also makes the transmission plan (incorporated in the RUPTL) impossible to comprehend from an outside perspective, as without indication of future generation location (among other relevant factors), future electricity flows, and related transmission upgrade requirements cannot be assessed.

While the RUPTL is meant to translate the long-term policy plan into actionable investments, the lack of transparency and level of discrepancy between plans fails to provide a reliable pathway to potential investors. It was not the aim of our assessment to perform a full-fledged assessment of gaps in the planning process. However, it is evident that the RUPTL is not sufficiently reliable to stakeholders. As such, the current RUPTLs can be (and are) too easily dismissed as representing the opinion of a limited set of decision makers of what the hypothetical future of Indonesia's electricity system might entail, rather than a plan to be implemented. The RUPTL therefore fails as a tool to mobilize timely and efficient investment at the required scale. In this environment, irrational investments seem to have arisen, depending on the location, leading to infrastructure gaps, infrastructure surplus and/or other mismatches. In consequence, there is a need to improve the planning process.

Box 1:   Principles to Develop Accurate Investment Plans

Evidence suggests there are several main principles a planner needs to adhere to in order to develop accurate investment plans. The plan has to be in line with relevant policy objectives, rules, and regulations such as reliability, costs, or environmental performance and social factors (e.g., electrification targets). The time horizon for the plan is important as this horizon defines the benefits, costs, and uncertainties associated with the assets. A ten-year to twenty-year time horizon is commonly applied, with longer timelines benefitting more CAPEX-intense infrastructures. Good data and a resource capability assessment is at the heart of accurate investment plans. Especially at times of rapid innovation, the changing capabilities and costs of new technologies are as important as capturing fuel price volatility. Technology changes and their implications on energy supply costs can be so rapid that the updating frequency has to reflect these changes and their impact on the planning results. Planning processes must not only use the most current, but also the best locally available sources of data. Transparency is required for third parties to review and contribute to the data used, as well as the methods and models applied in the plan. The development of load forecasts and scenarios are commonly the first key steps in the planning process. Plans should include all relevant assets, i.e. supply-side infrastructure as well as demand-side technologies and energy efficiency technologies.

As part of the risk management, the plan should include multiple scenarios of possible future developments. A clear methodology is needed to identify and select portfolios of assets to deliver on the requirements of these scenarios, whilst adhering to public policy objectives and reduce associated investment risks.

Source: International Renewable Energy Agency. 2018. *Insights on Planning for Power System Regulators*. Abu Dhabi.

Enhancing the process for electricity sector planning in Indonesia needs to entail changes to the legal foundation, institutional set-up, and possibly the methodologies used.

The 2009 Electricity Law requires the development of the RUKN, while ministerial decisions establish further rules for its development, e.g., the 3-year review cycle and the roles of MEMR. Despite the RUPTL's legal foundation, there are significant consequences to the relevance of the RUPTL. Stakeholders, including government, are left without any reference points for the aims and processes of the plan. Furthermore, the main stakeholders will lack clarity of and authority for their roles in the formulation, approval, and implementation of the program. Consequently, stakeholders perceive the RUPTL as an informal plan at best. Evidence suggests that informal plans are far less likely to be implemented in the form of specific investment.

While it will not be the role for a planning authority to establish the legal foundation, the lack of this foundation significantly reduces the impact a planning authority could potentially have on the efficient implementation of a plan.

In the Indonesian context, PLN holds the most comprehensive and in-depth expertise to develop electricity plans. Beyond PLN, there is no other institution in Indonesia which holds the required planning capacities. PLN holds competencies in some of the most relevant positions of the Indonesian electricity supply business and is by far Indonesia's most dominant electricity service provider. At the same time, PLN acts as a single buyer to IPPs. Given its significance to the Indonesian electricity supply industry, PLN is the "natural candidate" when it comes to the development of a relevant electricity sector plan.

This assessment has not revealed any reasons as to why PLN's function as central planner should be discontinued. If a relevant plan is to be produced in the future, a change in the institutional set-up and methodologies to develop the RUPTLs seems inevitable. In parallel to the amendment of the legal foundation as discussed above, a neutral planning authority needs to be capable of enhancing the relevance of the RUPTLs to stakeholders other than PLN. The inclusion of such a body should initially be able to function as a moderator in the process to develop and approve the RUPTLs, including generation and transmission.

Assuming an initial lack of expert staff, a newly implemented planning authority should initially focus on the planning process. Over time, that authority can learn about the key aspects (methodologies, tools, and data) which could benefit from an in-depth review of subject matter details using in-house capabilities (e.g., demand forecasting, technology evaluation, risk management). The initial focus on the process will ensure that all relevant laws, regulations, and policy targets are being followed; that PLN as the central planner follows the main principles for good planning; and that all stakeholders to the plan are provided the opportunity to contribute to the final results. The authority will not judge on the result of the RUPTL, but on whether the planning process was sound.

The neutrality of the authority responsible to ensure relevance of the RUPTL is essential in the Indonesian context, as there remains a lack of competition for the market between generators, and thus, a lack of choices for consumers. Neutral oversight can be a powerful tool to mitigate stakeholders' impressions about a plan primarily serving PLN's interest. At the same time, neutrality can also enhance stakeholders' confidence in the RUPTL by ensuring that decisions are not unduly influenced by political pressure. While it is normal and appropriate for politics worldwide to influence planning, a neutral planning body can ensure that political influence is raised in a transparent manner and in line with policy and planning objectives, including the final selection of infrastructure assets to be developed. Following the examples from other parts of the world, it is advisable to allocate these planning functions to a regulatory body.

Box 2:   Lessons from the Formulation of Transmission Network Development Plan

Driven by decarbonization targets, the German electricity system is undergoing significant changes. The German electricity system has matured over time, with gross electricity demand only modestly fluctuating at levels between 560 to 620 terawatt-hours per year, for 2 decades. Peak demand usually occurs during wintertime with 82 gigawatts as reported maximum during the same timeframe.

In parallel, policy measures have effectively supported the uptake of renewable resources such as wind and solar PV. The contribution of renewables has increased from a 7% share of gross electricity demand in 1998 to 43% in 2018. This change has resulted and will continue to result in a significant need to restructure and expand the electricity transmission infrastructure in the German electricity system. Having surpassed a 20% share in electricity demand in 2010, German policymakers revised the existing legislation to institutionalize a binding TNDP. This plan responded to an ever-growing need for a comprehensive and transparent planning process that would build the foundation for transmission infrastructure investment.

The legal foundation requires German transmission system operators (TSOs) to produce a transmission network development plan (TNDP) in two steps: first through the development of a scenario framework and second through the development of the actual TNDP. In both cases, the TSOs seek regulatory approval for draft documents. As part of the planning process, the TSOs are obliged to publish the draft reports, including all the background data, methods, and tools, for public consultation. The final regulatory approval takes into consideration the initial draft report, amendments resulting from public consultation, as well as findings from internal needs assessments. The legal foundation also prescribes the timelines for the advancing through the planning process. Both the scenario framework as well as the TNDP are to be updated every two years and apply to a timeframe of ten to fifteen years ahead.

continued on next page

Box 2 *continued*

The TNDP process can be regarded as effective from different views. TSOs as well as political decision-makers use the TNDP to communicate the need to build new infrastructure (down to each single infrastructure measure) with the wider public. TSOs also use the outcomes of the TNDP for seeking accelerated regulatory approvals, thereafter, being it for cost recovery and adjustment of the regulated asset base, or for supporting environmental impact assessments, land acquisition, and building permit processes. Similarly, the regulatory body uses the TNDP to streamline internal approval processes and to monitor the scope and timing of investment implementation. Since 2011, when the first TNDP was published, the regulatory body has continuously enhanced its in-house expertise. The knowledge is now at a level where it is comparable, in some instances even more advanced, in comparison to the knowledge of the TSO as planning entities. For the wider public, the emergency of the TNDP has brought transparency to a formerly foreclosed process: a formally unclear background for transmission investment proposals was replaced by an evidence-based process.

Over time, the TNDP has become one of the most relevant policy documents in the German electricity system. The TNDP is widely regarded as transparent, comprehensive, technology-neutral, and innovative; as well as an effective instrument to advance timely transmission infrastructure investment in the German electricity sector. The plan also allows stakeholders to directly comprehend the consequences of changing public policies on infrastructure needs as well as system costs.

The neutrality of the regulatory body as an approving agency provides all stakeholders with sufficient confidence in the accuracy of the plan.

Source: Bundesnetzagentur. 2020. *Establishing Requirements.* Bonn.

Facilitating Off-Grid Electricity Supply

The last mile of electrification is very often the most expensive. In the Indonesian context the last mile is similar to the remaining amount of households without access to electricity, or without the ability to pay for it. Data varies in regard to the current electrification rate, which has been reported to be between 88.2% in 2016 to 97.1% in 2017 (World Bank, 2018). Irrespective of the actual electrification rate and resulting uncertainty whether Indonesia is 11.5 percentage points or 2.4 percentage points away from the 2020 electrification target, the last decades' progress is remarkable. The progress was centered on PLN as the provider and operator for off-grid solutions, with funding from the national budget (using the so-called "utility model"). Consumer rates in off-grid locations have been kept at the same rate grid-connected consumers pay. As such, off-grid rates have mostly been cross-subsidized. Indonesia has a dedicated regulation to advance non-PLN mini-grid development (private model through Regulation 38/2016). Nevertheless, there are only a few examples in Indonesia where private investors have developed and operated mini-grid solutions, such as the Sinar Siwo Mego electricity cooperative which served 72,000 consumers in Lampung. The Sinar Siwo Mego electricity cooperative ceded operations after the governor revoked their license, responding to growing discomfort in the local population as service tariffs have been higher than the PLN on-grid tariffs.

While the private model has not been operationalized to its full potential, the utility model has come increasingly under pressure as PLN's financial abilities are constrained (see sub-section 4 on tariff setting) and as new technology solutions challenge the commonly applied solutions (i.e., grid connection or diesel generators). The situation is exacerbated by the fact that the remaining population without access to electricity lives in remote locations (World Bank, 2018) and the fact that the target year for achieving almost universal electrification is 2020. Both aspects—location and time—will make it more costly to achieve the target. The overall situation may call for an updated approach toward electrification in Indonesia, a strategy which would reliably and efficiently complement electrification through the national grid with the growing use of non-PLN models to develop and operate mini-grids (e.g., from 10 kilowatts upwards), microgrids (e.g., 1 to 10 kilowatts) and stand-alone systems (e.g., single households solar photovoltaic systems; 10 to 150 watts).

As this segment of the industry has benefited from the development of small-scale energy applications (such as renewables and storage), light-handed regulatory approaches are common as electrification often builds on smaller-scale projects and initiatives whose efficiency may be reduced from regulatory burdens. In most cases, regulatory approaches encompass licensing and registration, determination of the least-cost means of electrifying unserved areas (e.g., by grid extension or isolated mini-grids), tariff setting, and what happens when the main grid reaches the mini-grid. Licensing requirements are often only applied from a certain project size onwards (e.g., 1 megawatt and above), while smaller systems often only require registration. Because of the cost structures, tariffs for mini-grids are often set at levels above the tariffs for urban customers connected to the national grid. In this context, costs vary widely even among mini-grid solutions, so that mini-grid developers are often allowed to propose a tariff structure and rate appropriate for the project, with the regulator to approve. Again, depending on the project size, small projects may be exempt from prior regulatory review or approval of retail tariffs. To prepare for the time when the main grid arrives, regulators can provide prior guidance to the industry for cases such as continued operations of the mini-grid following the arrival of the main grid, ceased operations of the mini-grid, changed operations of the mini grid, asset transfer from the mini-grid owner to the main grid, and/ or asset relocation of the mini-grid.

Infrastructure Procurement

PLN acts as the main supplier of electricity, owning around 60% of electricity generation assets and all transmission infrastructure (PWC, 2018). The remaining capacity is owned and operated by IPPs, selling all electricity directly to PLN at prices established through PPAs.

Efficient infrastructure procurement for PLN-owned assets as well as for IPPs is essential to deliver timely and efficient investment. Given the structural set-up with PLN as a single buyer and the involvement of a significant and increasingly growing role of IPPs in the Indonesian electricity market, contracting processes and economic regulation should be well designed. However, our analysis has revealed a lack of oversight and enforcement to level the playing field for contract formulation between IPPs and PLN and may suggest further inefficiencies with regard to the overall procurement process. These aspects may indicate a sub-optimal policy and regulatory framework for procuring infrastructure through independent producers, a framework which also may fall short on price determination for PLN-owned assets (see subsection 4 on tariff setting). While it is outside the scope of this work to review the entire procurement process in Indonesia, such an assessment may be beneficial to optimize infrastructure investment conditions.

A well-designed procurement framework in single-buyer markets consists of the following tasks:

1. *Linkage between investment plan and procurement process* with the aim to define future procurement actions planned and required on a single-asset level; classify, if needed, the set of assets to be procured with or without competition between PLN and other potential proponents; support regulatory approval on the need to procure certain assets; and initiate procurement. The more detailed the future procurement actions are within or following the investment plan, the clearer a signal to IPPs and to those responsible for financing power system investments will be about the timing and kind of investment needed. Public

investors such as the MOF will find it easier to accept investment projects related to the investment plan, as these have been scrutinized against key economic indicators and other criteria. The observed performance relative to this action plan can also serve as a reference point for regulators to monitor and scrutinize resource procurement decisions and tariff setting processes.

Box 3:   Investment Plan and Procurement Process in Brazil and South Africa

In Brazil, the need for procurement is established through the annual electricity expansion plans developed by the Energy Research Office, which is dedicated to energy planning. As the country's energy regulator, the National Electric Energy Agency is responsible for the implementation of the plan by facilitating the procurement of new projects. Through this process, over 50,000 kilometers of new transmission have been built since the early 2000s (Brattle, 2014).

In South Africa, the Integrated Resource Plan (IRP) identifies generation investment requirements, including the preferred future energy mix. The minister of energy, in consultation with the national electricity regulator, can determine capacity procurement requirements. In this way, the determination gives effect to assets identified in the IRP. Since 2010 the newly established Independent Power Producers Procurement Programme (IPPPP) Office is responsible for managing the procurement as well as for contract monitoring aspects. The establishment of the procurement process and the IPPPP office is regarded as a successful response to overcome electricity supply constraints since 2008 (IPP Office South Africa, 2019).

Source: IPP Office South Africa. 2019. *Independent Power Producer Procurement Programme.* Centurion; The Brattle Group. 2014. *Competition in Transmission Planning and Development: Current Status and International Experience.* Washington, DC.

2. *Identification of the scope for competition* to define whether and to what extent a form of competitive procurement will be applied for assets to be procured. This describes the extent the incumbent utility will be directly assigned to build, own, and operate assets, and in the scope of assets to be built, owned, and operated following a form of competitive selection. The allocation of assets toward direct assignment or competitive procurement is commonly decided along the lines of a pre-defined list of criteria, such as the nature of the service provision (reliability, commercial, public policy), time sensitivity, size, location, and nature of the investment (new-build, replacement, upgrades or technology) associated to a specific asset. In some cases, incumbent utilities have the right of first refusal to exempt assets from competitive procurement. To gain these rights on a case-by-case basis, incumbent utilities are often required to file an application to receive that right.

3. *Licensing* is commonly done prior to the initiation of procurement. Licensing effectively seeks to ensure that any company intending to engage in any type of business in the industry is deemed reliable and capable. Licenses are often provided upon application with a government institution.

Box 4:   Nigerian Electricity Regulatory Commission Performs Licensing Task

Established by law, the Nigerian Electricity Regulatory Commission (NERC) issues licenses to interested entities in the field of generation, transmission, system operation, distribution or trading. NERC scrutinizes applicants against clearly defined legal, financial, technical criteria (NERC, 2018).

Source: Government of Nigeria, Nigerian Electricity Regulatory Commission (NERC). 2010. *Regulation No: NERC-R-0110A on the Application for Licenses (Generation, Transmission, System Operations, Distribution & Trading).* Abuja.

4. *Procurement* to contract generation and transmission capacity. Various procurement models are applied in practice, and the choice of which model to adopt often depends on a number of factors, including (but not limited to) expediency, technology and market depth, regulatory control quality, flexibility to amend requirements during the procurement process, amount of individual projects to be procured, allowed procurement complexity, and process predictability. Commonly applied procurement models include direct assignment, bilateral negotiations, feed-in-tariffs, and competitive tenders (auctions). In short, auctions are commonly applied when competitive price determination is necessary. For several reasons, auctions are also the preferred model for development banks. Bilateral negotiations are often used in the context of project expansion investment and are also a result of unsolicited bids offered from the promoter to the offtaker. Feed-in tariffs are used to support technology-specific development at a fixed price, and often establish a timeframe in which projects can be developed and contracted.

Box 5:   Brazil's Experiences in Electricity Procurement through Auctions

Brazil is using auctions for the procurement of all types of generation assets. Auctions are differentiated by type of service to be procured. Auction timings are set by the Ministry of Mines and Energy, with guidelines for the auction systematics provided by the National Electric Energy Agency. In 2018, several auctions have been conducted to procure energy, assigning "quantity" contracts for hydropower and wind projects; and "availability" contracts for biomass, coal, and natural gas projects. For new projects, price caps were set at prices between 60 USD/megawatt-hour (MWh) (wind) to 81 USD/MWh (thermal). The auction resulted in the procurement of 2.1 gigawatts of new capacity, broken down into eleven hydropower plants (average price: 48 USD/MWh), two sugarcane biomass projects, one gas-fired power plant (47 USD/MWh), and forty-eight windpower plants (24 USD/MWh) (EPE, 2018).

Source: Asian Development Bank.

Source: Energy Research Office (EPE). 2018. *Brazilian Electricity Auctions in 2018.* Rio de Janeiro.

5. *Power purchase agreements* mark the end of the procurement process through contract formulation between buyer and supplier of electricity. The PPAs define obligations related to the sales and purchases of the power generated, including price and amounts, over a specific time. It is very common that PPAs further define a long list of rights and requirements between the contracting parties, as well as technical specifications for the facility procured. International Finance Corporation (IFC 1998) provides more details on the design features of PPAs.

6. *Prudence review* to determine whether an asset has been constructed or implemented as proposed. Common criteria to be assessed include implementation management practices, costs, and diligence. Prudence reviews can use a comparison between actual utility performance against a previously defined set of goals.

While the Indonesian electricity laws address a wide range of the abovementioned tasks, our analysis has revealed that the current framework is being used inefficiently. Continuous changes to standard PPA contracts are cumbersome for IPPs, as these changes make internal PPA assessments more time consuming and less reliable to IPPs. This escalates administrative costs significantly and can be an impediment to interested parties. Furthermore, the practice indicates a lack of reliable and impartial conflict resolution between IPPs and PLN.

In theory and practice, electricity regulators take many roles along the lines of the abovementioned tasks. These include the monitoring and enforcement of projects resulting from the investment plan; inclusion of actual project costs into tariffs; licensing; partially defining and implementing a selected (set of) procurement models, including bid evaluation, contribution to PPA design and complaint management; as well as project implementation prudence review.

We suggest the newly formed Indonesian electricity regulatory body to be accordingly empowered to avoid shortcomings in the procurement process in the future.

Efficient Cost Recovery and Cost Allocation

Our assessment has revealed strong indications for electricity tariffs in Indonesia being set at levels below the economic costs of service provision. The widespread opinion among stakeholders strongly suggests political decision-making is interfering with rational electricity tariff setting processes. This interference can be regarded as a systemic failure to establish a political consensus on how to protect parts of society that cannot afford higher prices.

At the same time, the current tariffs are likely to lead to a shortfall in electricity infrastructure investment while the timely implementation of a large investment program is required to meet the growing needs of the sector. With rising fuel prices, operational costs are expected to rise, exacerbating the impacts of missing cost-reflectivity without countermeasures.

Summarizing the main arguments made by the World Bank (World Bank, 2018) in this context, significant impacts are possible if the current situation persists into the future. In short, PLN, as the main asset owner and investor in the Indonesian electricity sector, will find itself in a situation where the gap between its cash flow and service costs widens. This could put PLN in a situation where its financial performance diminishes and its financing costs escalate due to higher risk premiums to be paid to prudent financiers.

Under this scenario, in order to maintain sufficient investment activity, either through PLN directly, or as a creditworthy offtaker to independent power producers, the government of Indonesia would have to further increase financial support to the sector. This could reverse the efforts and progress made since 2012 in reducing

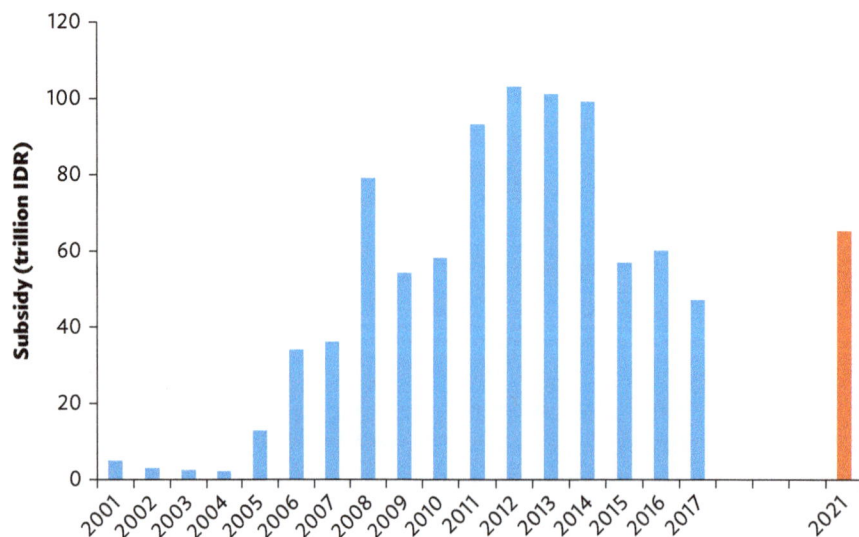

Figure 5:   Subsidies Paid by the Government of Indonesia to the Electricity Sector

Source: Authors, data and adapted from World Bank, 2018.

electricity subsidies, potentially leading to a required annual government subsidy of around IDR65 trillion (USD4.73 billion) per year by 2021 (World Bank, 2018). Growing levels of financial dependence from the state budget may also negatively influence PLN's objective decision-making processes.

If the Government of Indonesia is keen to reverse the trend of subsidy development, a tariff increase is the only option left. Given the current market circumstances and infrastructure needs in the Indonesian context, progress will only be possible by introducing tariffs that reflect the economic cost of electricity service provision.

Managing tariffs is a complex and continuous undertaking, and the decision-making process will be subject to influence driven by the interest of various stakeholders. PLN will benefit from higher tariffs as almost any upward tariff change enhances PLN's financial performance and may reduce its borrowing costs. Investors will also find it easier to negotiate PPAs with accurate prices and may assign lower financial risks to PLN as offtaker. At the same time, PLN and investors are likely to try to influence tariff-setting decisions to maximize their own benefits. The MOF is also very likely to benefit from more cost-reflective tariffs as shrinking subsidy requirements from the electricity sector can free up financial resources, which can be potentially reallocated to other sectors of the Indonesian economy. Customers can show mixed responses to increasing tariff levels, depending on the way cost reflectivity is pursued: tariff increases which are mostly allocated to customer groups with limited abilities to afford these cost increases will result in low levels of acceptance. The ability to manage the expectations and responses of different stakeholders will be a key driving factor in the behavior of the MEMR.

Arriving at such tariff levels is a multifaceted undertaking, requiring decision-making capabilities, and technical, economic, and social expertise, in addition to stakeholder management skills. It also requires continuous engagement and periodic review as part of an informed and rational tariff setting process. For the essential components, the management of these aspects can be supported through good regulatory decision-making.

Today, the Indonesian electricity sector builds on current administered service pricing. Changes to electricity tariffs require a presidential or government decree. The government has tried to limit the number of proposed changes, which has resulted in larger tariff increases at once instead of continuous adjustments. If the government arrives at the conclusion and consensus to develop a rational electricity tariff-setting strategy, the use of a regulatory body will provide greater transparency and trust in the tariff determinations. A high-quality regulatory body would be a competent actor in this field, whose impartial tariff recommendations can provide strong justifications and support for rational decisions made by the President of the government. With a growing reputation and trust within the sector and political environment, a transfer of ultimate decision-making rights

Box 6:   Path to Cost-Reflective Tariffs by the Kosovo Energy Regulatory Office

The Energy Regulatory Office (ERO) was established in 2004 and continued tariff setting in 2007 with the second price review for electricity services. The second price review was the start to phase out existing subsidies to consumers at all voltage levels. The second price review tariff setting methodology included a reduction of allowed costs within the calculated tariffs, equaling the operating subsidies paid to electricity supply companies from the state budget (ERO, 2007). The allocation of costs featured a cross-subsidization from high voltage to low voltage consumers to protect households. Therefore, this approach targeted a cost reduction for high voltage consumers' prices to economic costs in this consumer segment, without allowing the full subsidy recovery through higher tariffs with lower voltage consumers. This process was repeated until the sixth price review in 2012, which ultimately prepared the ground to reach cost-reflective tariffs in all consumer groups by 2014 (ERO, 2012).

Sources: ERO. 2007. *Annual Report*. Pristina; and ERO. 2012. *Annual Report*. Pristina.

to the regulatory body could enhance transparency, make decisions more direct, and eliminate stakeholders' uncertainty on possible political interference in the future. The delegation of decision-making authority to a regulatory body could also be a solution to a political stalemate between different political parties or ministries.

Independent of the institutional arrangements of decision-making, decisions to establish rational tariffs will benefit from technical, economic, and social expertise. The standard principle is to set tariffs that allow the utility to earn a reasonable rate of return after expenses which include the capital expenses (CAPEX), interest on debt, and a return on equity in addition to the operating expenses (OPEX) that encompass the labor, fuel, taxes, and other recurring costs.

- Functional and jurisdictional allocation of costs is the first consideration of the tariff setting process in order to clearly separate costs between generation and transmission and other parts of the sector, and to allow for geographic delineation (e.g., between unconnected islands).

- Setting the revenue requirement is the primary aspect of concern, as below-requirement settings will impede investment in the long run. The revenue requirement is described as CAPEX + Rate of Return + OPEX = Revenue Requirement.

- In the context of setting the revenue requirement, the rate year defines whether the data used for setting the tariff is based on real (historical) data, forecasted (future) data or a combination of both. Also, it has to be decided whether that year's start date, end date, or annual average (the latter being the most common approach) is used to determine the costs.

- A significant part of the entire revenue requirement, the rate of return, provides the investors' incentive to do business. It is most common that the rate of return will enable investors to attract additional capital under efficient management and reflect the level of risk for doing business in the specified environment. Different rates are set for the different forms of equity (often applying standard methodologies such as the capital asset pricing model) and debt. In this context, the share of equity and debt is commonly set through a maximum level of equity or a weighting.

- OPEX can vary continuously and unpredictability and is often treated as (full) pass-through by using adjustment mechanisms. CAPEX relates to the depreciation of facilities, allowing amortization of investment over a specific time frame.

- Once the overall tariff is determined, the allocation of costs through tariff differentiation between customer classes is often the next part of the tariff-setting decision. There are many ways to determining tariffs for each customer class, considering that most of the customers already differ by the way they distinguish between classes. Often, regulatory bodies consider the results of alternative ways for cost allocation when determining the ultimate tariff cost delineation.

- The design of rates follows the cost allocation and describes whether customers will be charged by consumption (kilowatt-hour) or peak demand (kilowatt), and the change of these charges (e.g., based on time of use or variations by season).

- Evidence suggests that standard regulatory approaches for tariff setting do not necessarily lead to additional economic costs (for either CAPEX or OPEX). The regulated utility often uses its depth of information advantages to influence regulatory decision-making to be in their favor, resulting in less stringent cost-efficiency requirements. In response, cost regulations have developed to make regulated utilities' performance relevant to cost approvals. This has been accomplished by performing in-depth prudence reviews to determine if a facility was built in an economical fashion or by linking results from long-term planning exercises (volume and costs) with the tariff setting process.

Pricing electricity to protect the poor seems necessary in Indonesia, but the way this protection is being administered and communicated can result in substantial differences in the accuracy and acceptance of the overall tariff-setting process. It seems beneficial to openly and broadly communicate the objectives of the tariff-setting process (e.g., to achieve cost reflectivity while protecting vulnerable customers). If and when overall cost-reflectivity of the tariffs is to be considered, the practice of compensation (for the poor) has to be evidence-based to avoid inaccurate levels of compensation, weak targeting, and/or almost universal compensation. The required re-distribution of burden can be achieved through various alternatives such as lifeline rates, provisions for uncollectible accounts, or waivers for the basic monthly charges. Indonesia's social database and its regular revision and application to the list of subsidized households has been a first step toward evidence-based electricity subsidies.

In this context, a high-quality regulatory body can take into consideration communication from the government and contrive targeted strategies aimed at persuading specific constituencies or groups of citizens on the merits of specific policy prescriptions, as well as target group identification for protection measures, to apply the right methodology to achieve accurate levels of compensation.

Establishing the Indonesian Electricity Regulatory Body

Legal Aspects

As a basic principle, the establishment of any public institution should be based on law that is clearly written in the form of (i) an expressed mandate or instruction that specifically assigns certain tasks to a particular institution. One example from the transport sector would be the Indonesian Toll Road Authority (BPJT) which was specifically mandated under Article 45 of Law No. 38 of 2004 on Roads or (ii) a general mandate to the government for a certain responsibility.

Asshiddiqie (Asshiddiqie: 2006, 49) provides useful classification of four levels of national institutions based on their sources of establishment under Indonesian law:

- *Institutions established based on the Indonesian Constitution.* These include President, vice-president, People's Consultative Assembly, Supreme Court, DPR, Regional House of Representatives, State Audit Board, and Judicial Commission. The authorities of these institutions are set out in the Constitution and further detailed in laws. Further, since the Indonesian Constitution is the highest regulation in Indonesia's hierarchy of laws, the dissolution of these institutions would require strict procedures of amending the Indonesian Constitution.

- *Institutions established based on law.* These include the Attorney General's Office, Corruption Eradication Commission, General Election Commission, and Bank of Indonesia. Under the Indonesian Constitution, lawmaking or legislative power falls under the authority of DPR subject to the President's approval. An institution that is formed through law obtains its authority from the law; therefore, dissolution or adjustment to such an institution can only be done through the applicable lawmaking process.

- *Formed based on Government Regulation or Presidential Regulation.* These include Electricity Market Supervisory Agency (BPTL), Special Task Force for Upstream Oil and Gas Business Activities (SKK Migas), National Consumer Protection Agency, and Statistics Regulatory Body.

- *Formed based on Ministerial Regulation.* These include the BPJT under the Ministry of Public Works and Housing, Indonesian Telecommunication Regulatory Body under the Ministry of Communication and Informatics, and Commodity Futures Trading Supervisory Agency under the Ministry of Trade. A ministry may also establish an institution to support the function of that ministry. Such an institution may be in the form of a body or agency, trustee, institution, or specific and ad hoc committee that will have a direct institutional relationship with the relevant ministry. However, the establishment of an independent regulatory body through ministerial regulations must (usually) be referred to first in the relevant law.

There are several key differences to note in determining to which sources of law the establishment of a regulatory body should be based on (see Table 2).

Table 2:   Comparison between Sources of Law

	Law	Government Regulation	Presidential Regulation
Hierarchy	Above Government Regulation	Above Presidential Regulation	Below Government Regulation
Source of Authority	Rule-making authority and policy-making authority	Rule-making authority	Executive power to administer the government
Purpose	1) Carry out policy-making authority. 2) Carry out rule-making authority.	Implement provisions of the law.	1) Implement provisions of the law. 2) Implement provisions of the Government Regulation. 3) Carry out the presidential executive power.
Procedures based on PR 87 of 2014	1) Preparation of draft laws may come from the President, DPR, or Regional Representatives Council. 2) A draft law which comes from the President is prepared by a ministry/relevant agency. 3) The draft law is then submitted to the national legislation program by DPR. 4) The draft law must be accompanied by an academic document. 5) The chair of DPR shall give notice of the draft law and circulate it to the members of the DPR to be discussed in the Great Assembly, which will have 2 levels of hearing: (a) Standing Committee meetings, Joint Standing Committee meetings, Legislation Council meetings, Budget Committee meetings, or Special Committee meetings; and (b) the Great Assembly which will be continued with a vote.[a] 6) The DPR shall decide whether the draft law is approved, rejected, or approved with certain amendments in the subsequent Great Assembly. 7) The relevant initiator (ministry/non-ministerial institution/other institution) shall harmonize, perfect, and finalize the draft law and report to the relevant ministry/institution before concluding a substantial approval for the draft law.	1) The relevant ministry to prepare the Government Regulation draft program. 2) The relevant ministry to register for the Government Regulation drafting program. 3) Coordination meeting between ministries/nonministerial agencies to be conducted within 14 days from registration. 4) Coordination meeting for finalization of the Government Regulation drafting program. 5) Government Regulation drafting program to be stipulated by a Presidential Decree. 6) Relevant ministry to prepare the Government Regulation draft by forming a committee. 7) Public consultation. 8) President to enact the Government Regulation draft.	1) Drafting by initiator (i.e., minister or head of a nonministerial institution who proposes the Presidential Regulation).[c] 2) Consultation with relevant ministry/nonministerial agency or other relevant agencies. 3) Consultation results may be delivered to the President to be enacted.

continued on next page

Table 2: *continued*

Law	Government Regulation	Presidential Regulation
8) DPR will conduct a voting for the enactment of the law.		
9) DPR will then deliver the approved draft law to the President to be enacted.[b]		

DPR = Dewan Perwakilan Rakyat (House of Representatives).
[a] Government of Indonesia. 2011. *Law No. 12*. Jakarta. Article 66 *juncto* Article 67 provides that the first level reading will be conducted in Standing Committee meetings, Joint Standing Committee meetings, Legislation Council meetings, Budget Committee meetings, or Special Committee meetings. After that, the second level reading will be conducted in a plenary session.
[b] Government of Indonesia. 2014. *Presidential Regulation No. 87/2014*. Jakarta.
[c] Footnote b, Article 1(14).
Source: Authors, based on Law No.12/2011 and Presidential Regulation No. 87/2014.

If we are focusing on finding the strongest legal foundation as the basis of the regulatory body, its establishment through a law would be the best scenario, as a law represents the highest hierarchy of power and the most sound source of authority only second to the Indonesian Constitution. However, the absence of an explicit establishment of a regulatory body in the electricity sector in the 2009 Electricity Law might become a hurdle in proposing the enactment of the regulatory body through a Government Regulation or a Presidential Regulation because, as we understand that in other sectors, the establishment of an independent regulatory body is usually explicitly mentioned in the relevant Law which will be further regulated by a Government Regulation and/or Presidential Regulation.

This path is in line with the general concept that Government Regulation and Presidential Regulation are both intended to set out further detailed implementation of their stipulations to provide more practical and operational implementation. Fortunately, the executive body (President) is also embedded with the power to enact laws as part of its own executive power. Two exemplary cases of the establishment of a regulatory body by virtue of Presidential Regulation are (i) the establishment of SKK Migas through the issuance of Presidential Regulation No. 9/2013 and (ii) the establishment of the State Administration Agency, whose creation was previously stipulated by virtue of Government Regulation No. 30 of 1957 on State Administration Agency (which was later revoked by Government Regulation No. 5 of 1971 and replaced by Presidential Regulation No. 20 of 1989 and Government Regulation No. 79 of 2018 on State Administration Agency). These agencies were both established without any underlying higher law.

Based on the above discussion, formation of the regulatory body can be done through issuance of either a law, Government Regulation or Presidential Regulation. These regulatory sources would be able to establish an independent regulatory body without any explicit mandate in the underlying higher regulations (though this might be a bit more problematic for a government regulation as we only have a single precedent for such enactment without an underlying law). For ministerial regulation, due to its duty to implement certain government policies as mandated by higher regulations, it can only be used to establish a regulatory body if it is specifically authorized to by the underlying higher law or by a specific authority of the relevant ministry when granted by higher regulation.

In addition, if the regulatory body is established based on ministerial regulation, such an establishment can only be responsible to the relevant ministry, and its decision-making power will be exclusively subject to the approval of the relevant ministry. This difference is noted when comparing the BPJT, the regulatory body in toll road sector, with SKK Migas, the regulatory body in oil and gas sector.

While BPJT has the duty to prepare operational procedures for land procurement, the task of assembling the land is still the responsibility of Ministry of Public Works and Housing and particularly of regional governments. Moreover, despite having the authority to plan and implement construction as well as to perform operation and maintenance of toll road conducted by the toll road business entities, BPJT is not involved in the high-level planning of road networks because BPJT's mandate is limited to legal financial matters and promotion of dialogue necessary for boosting the accountability of regulatory process.

Contrastingly, SKK Migas' mandate includes carrying out the entire management of upstream oil and gas business activities through production sharing contracts, ensuring that the extraction of state-owned oil and gas natural resources provides the maximum benefits and revenue for the prosperity of Indonesian society.

In contrast with SKK Migas that directly reports to the President, BPJT is still under the authority of Ministry of Public Works and Housing, curtailing the range of BPJT's autonomy and power. Each of its decisions would have to be approved by Ministry of Public Works and Housing. In practice, this restrains BPJT's authority in its dealings with concessionaires and other ministries, making it an agency with minimal statutory power and real authority. For further details and comparison of other regulatory bodies, please refer to Table A1: Comparison of Regulatory Bodies in Indonesia.

Other than the source of its establishment, we should also consider the budgeting and/or funding factor. The determination of whether the establishment of the new regulatory body requires another budget allocation relies on whether the body would be established within the existing ministry (such as MEMR) or established as a new stand-alone body that directly reports to the executive body (President). The central government and DPR must jointly approve the national budget while the regional budget must be jointly approved by the relevant regional government and Regional House of Representatives to be ultimately approved by the central government (specifically the Ministry of Home Affairs) before implementation. It takes approximately a year to plan, draft, discuss, and adopt a budget at both the national and local level.

If the regulatory body is established under the Directorate General of Electricity, its budgeting process can be carried out along with the annual budgeting procedures of MEMR. But if the regulatory body is to be made as a stand-alone independent body outside MEMR, the procedures would have to be done in accordance with Government Regulation No. 90/2010 on Arrangement of Working Plan and Ministerial/ Institutional Budget.

According to Article 1 paragraph (2) of Government Regulation No. 90/2010, an institution is defined as a non-ministerial organization and another agency that is categorized as a state budget user, established to carry out certain tasks based on the Indonesian Constitution or other laws and regulations. Regardless of the budgeting procedures, the budgeting issue itself cannot be avoided, and the analysis on this issue must be further integrated into the overall analysis on deciding the basis for establishing the regulatory body.

The following tables provide an overview of the advantages and disadvantages of the establishment of the regulatory body through law, Government Regulation, and Presidential Regulation:

Table 3:   Legal Options for the Establishment of the Regulatory Body

	Law	Government Regulation	Presidential Regulation
Advantages	1) Creates very strong grounds for the establishment of the regulatory body. 2) Can only be amended by joint approval of the government and DPR, creating a sustainable regulatory environment for the regulatory body.	1) Has higher authority as a legal basis compared to Presidential Regulation. 2) Can be made without any approval from DPR. 3) While the authority to make a Government Regulation ultimately lies with the President, in practice, given the process of issuing a Government Regulation, its longevity is more sustainable compared to a Presidential Regulation even when President changes.	1) Has a simpler rule-making procedure compared to Government Regulation and law, and in any case, does not require DPR's approval. 2) There are numerous precedents for establishing regulatory bodies without definitive instructions from higher regulations.
Disadvantages	1) Requires political negotiation with DPR to issue the law. 2) Lengthy process to create the establishment.	1) There is a lack of precedent for establishing new regulatory bodies without definitive instruction from law. 2) More complicated rule-making procedure compared to Presidential Regulation.	1) Sustainability of the institution relies heavily on the discretion of President (if the President changes, the rule can also be easily revoked).

DPR = Dewan Perwakilan Rakyat (House of Representatives).

Source: Authors.

Based on the above description and the cited advantages and disadvantages, the following matrix summarizes the considerations in choosing the basis for the regulatory body establishment.

Table 4:   Consideration Matrix in Choosing the Legal Basis

No.	Aspects of Consideration	Law	Government Regulation	Presidential Regulation
1.	Time Efficiency	•	••	•••
2.	Simplicity of Procedure	•	•	•••
3.	Sustainability of the Regulatory Environment	•••	••	•
4.	Likelihood of Success	•	••	•••

Source: Authors.

Ensuring High-Quality Decision-Making and Efficient Task Management

Section 3 discussed the key tasks for an Indonesian electricity regulatory body, including infrastructure planning and procurement, as well as tariff setting. The set of tasks can change over time as new issues emerge, and so will the body's staffing, expertise, and decision-making processes. Even within a task, the role for the regulatory body may be subject to change, again requiring changes to the previously mentioned aspects.

Independent of the tasks and roles, for the Indonesian electricity regulatory body to deliver on its expectations, an enabling environment is required to support high-quality regulatory decision-making (as briefly introduced in Section 1 of this report).

Role clarity should be considered a key part of such an enabling environment as having clarity on the responsibilities of the organization will guide the regulators' staff, regulated entities, and citizens. This clarity will provide purpose and help to avoid or resolve overlaps and associated conflicts. The Indonesian Electricity Law would be the preferable law to clearly define, among others, the regulators' objectives, tasks, and roles. These designated responsibilities should be in line with the tasks and objectives to be achieved, e.g., the regulator would need to be legally empowered to approve the RUPTL in order to regulate investment planning in Indonesia credibly. For achieving effective outcomes, the regulator should, for example, be able to gather all relevant information and methods necessary to approve the investment plan.

Box 7:   The Transparent Development of Electricity Plan in the State of Georgia

The following provides a legal foundation that was used for the development of an electricity plan in the State of Georgia in the United States (State of Georgia, 1991, § 46-3A-2), which established the roles and responsibilities of the utility and planning authority.

(a)   On or before 31 January 1992, and at least every three years thereafter as may be determined by the commission, each utility shall file with the commission an integrated resource plan as described in this chapter.

(b)   Not more than 60 days after a utility has filed its plan, the commission shall convene a public hearing on the adequacy of the plan. At the hearing, any interested person may make comments to the commission regarding the contents and adequacy of the plan. After the hearing, the commission shall determine whether:

   (1)   The utility's forecast requirements are based on substantially accurate data and an adequate method of forecasting;

   (2)   The plan identifies and takes into account any present and projected reductions in the demand for energy which may result from measures to improve energy efficiency in the industrial, commercial, residential, and energy-producing sectors of the state; and

   (3)   The plan adequately demonstrates the economic, environmental, and other benefits to the state and to customers of the utility, associated with the following possible measures and sources of supply:

     (A)   Improvements in energy efficiency;

     (B)   Pooling of power;

     (C)   Purchases of power from neighboring states;

     (D)   Facilities which operate on alternative sources of energy;

     (E)   Facilities that operate on the principle of cogeneration or hydro-generation; and

     (F)   Other generation facilities and demand-side options.

(c)   Within 120 days after the filing of each integrated resource plan, the commission shall approve and adopt an integrated resource plan.

Source: Government of Georgia. 1991. *Georgia Code Title 46 Public Utilities and Public Transportation.*

Setting objectives will allow others to hold the regulator accountable for their performance. The degree of prescription in legislation determines the level of discretion the regulator will hold: a more principle-based legal framework will allow the regulator greater freedom and responsibilities to make decisions. Furthermore, the scope and depth of cooperation with other stakeholders should be determined, e.g., for the Indonesian regulator to seek approval from the President prior to determining electricity supply tariffs.

The integrity of regulatory processes is essential to build trust and general acceptance for decisions, and thus, impacting investment behavior. *Protecting against undue influence and maintaining the reliability of decisions* are the two main factors to consider when aiming for integrity. Keeping the Indonesian regulator at arm's length from the political sphere and the regulated entities will enhance public confidence in the regulator and support a level playing field between PLN as a state-owned company and private investors. If the regulator is established as a department within MEMR, the financial, organizational, and decision-making autonomy is best to be provided in the Electricity Law or at least within a framework agreement between MEMR and the regulator. At best, high-level staff, e.g., board members or senior agents, should not be involved in decisions related to previous employers, and the appointment and contract termination process for high-level staff should be explicitly stated in the Electricity Law. Communication between the regulator, the political sphere, and regulated entities should be made transparent. Furthermore, if the MEMR or the President directs the regulator, this direction should only be given in a transparent manner and within clearly defined boundaries. Using stakeholder input, empirical evidence and research as part of the decision-making process will further strengthen the trust and acceptance of regulatory decisions. Transparency about the information and methodologies used to arrive at specific regulatory decisions will strengthen the rule of law and support high-quality regulatory decision-making.

Regulating the (Indonesian) electricity industry requires an effective and functioning regulator, consisting of adequate *internal decision-making structures and a well-designed governing body*. Building on a clearly defined set of tasks, ideally as part of the Indonesian Electricity Law, the regulator would work within a clearly defined scope in coordination with the political sphere, but also within the institution. The latter aspect will determine the membership composition and split in responsibilities between the regulator's advisory and governing bodies and the head of the institution (e.g., chief executive officer and/or president). For strategic decisions, a multistakeholder advisory body consisting of formally designated political representatives could be considered a valuable tool. This body could be the guiding interface between the key technocratic decisions the regulator would take and the political sphere. In Indonesia, it could advise the regulator on acceptable thresholds which define vulnerable customers, and thus form the basis to identify the scope of cost-reflectivity to be achieved through tariff setting (see subsection 4 in Section 3). For day-to-day decision-making, internal governing board(s) could be established. Most relevant in this regard is to establish a board structure with multiple decision-makers to ensure that different experience and perspectives are included in regulatory decision-making and to enhance the institutional memory for tasks which require long-lasting involvement (such as tariff setting or investment planning). The governing bodies are best to consist of experts in their respective fields to eliminate undue influence from the political sphere. To maintain information exchange and avoid mistrust in the regulator's decisions, representatives from the political sphere and/or MEMR could be invited as observers to participate in meetings of the governing body.

Accountability and transparency are further aspects that can build trust in the regulatory decisions from the political sphere, to the regulated entities, and to the public. A system of accountability is required to hold the regulator accountable. This accountability would be ideally established between the regulator and the MEMR to define the regulator's performance indicators and assessment methodologies clearly. In this context, annual performance reporting can support legislative oversight. At the same time, transparency can not only provide information on a regulator's performance but also shape the outcome and acceptance of regulatory decisions. As discussed in Section 3, many of the key regulatory tasks in Indonesia, such as investment planning and tariff setting, can benefit from clearly defined stakeholder dialogue practices that are transparent. For example, the Indonesian Electricity Law could require the use of a clearly defined system for stakeholder dialogue in the context of approving the proposed investment plans.

When it comes to funding the regulator and its activities, the most important considerations are the impact of the funding level on the quality of the regulatory decision-making process as well as on the regulators' neutrality. Simplicity and adequacy are as important as transparency of the source of the funding. A mix of funding sources are available, including dedicated budget lines from government or the budget from the MEMR; regulatory fees; income from penalties and fines; and interest earned on investments and trust funds. In the Indonesian case, a dedicated budget line seems to be most suited to implement a regulator from scratch. Especially in the early years of regulation, regulatory fees would struggle with stakeholder's cash flow and acceptance of funding, from unclear understanding of the regulators' cost–benefit ratio. At the same time, a budget that significantly builds on penalties and fines is likely to result in uncertainty and a lack of financial means to pursue all regulatory tasks effectively. In case the regulator would be independent of MEMR, a dedicated budget line from the government is required; otherwise, a line from the MEMR budget should be clearly defined in a regulatory agreement between MEMR and the regulator. The longer the budget line, the less prone the regulator would be to uncertainty and political influence.

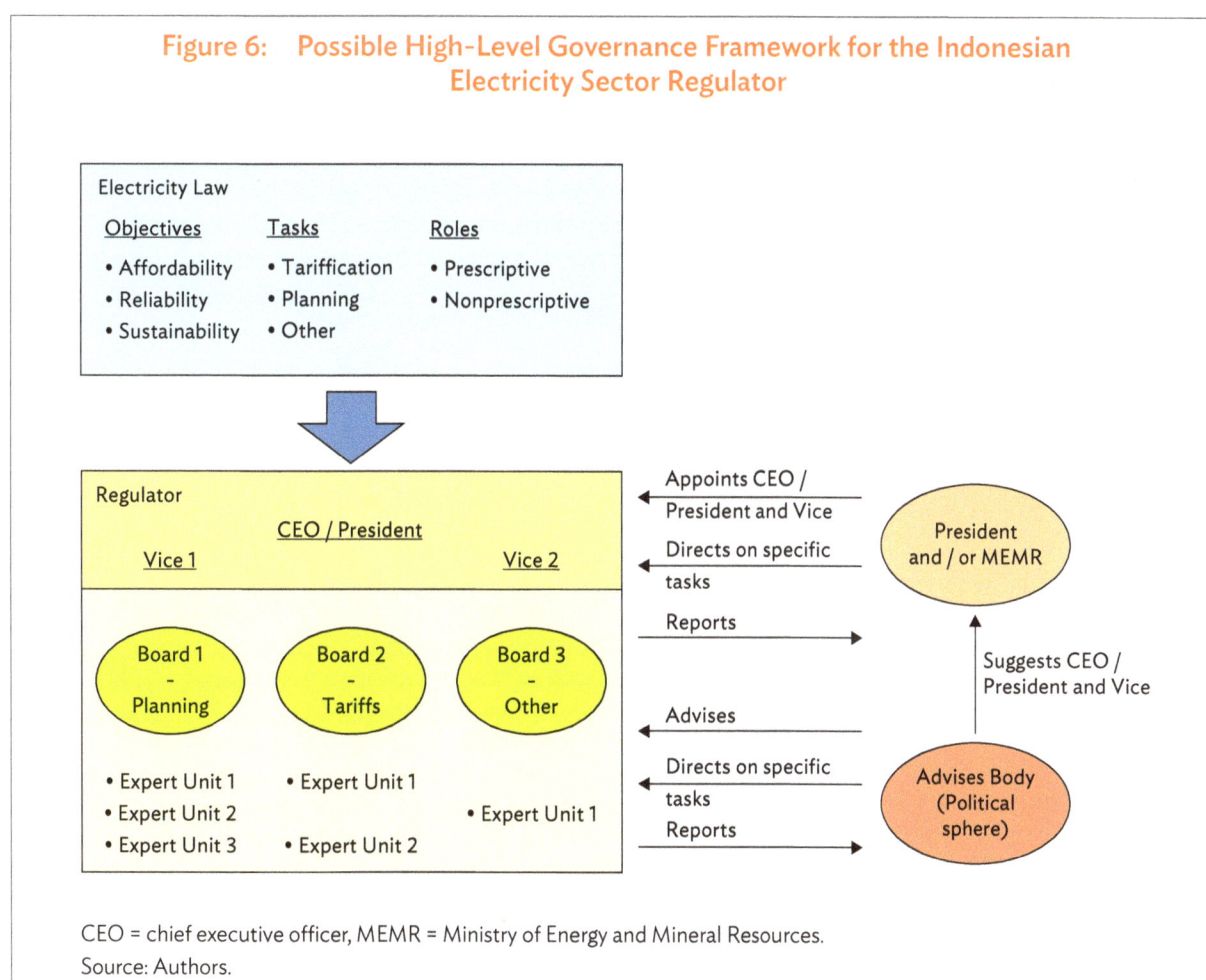

Figure 6:   Possible High-Level Governance Framework for the Indonesian Electricity Sector Regulator

CEO = chief executive officer, MEMR = Ministry of Energy and Mineral Resources.
Source: Authors.

Managing the tasks, as discussed in Section 1 will require a specifically designed environment in which the Indonesian electricity regulator operates as well as with a staffing complement of experts.

In Section 3, we propose the regulator to ensure stakeholder input and approval of the RUPTL in order to make the investment plan credible.

The existing legal foundation from the 2009 Electricity Law has to be critically reviewed and potentially updated to reflect the new regulatory roles. It will be essential to require the regulator to establish a reliable and consultative environment for engagement, which can be used by stakeholders to influence views and draft proposals made by PLN (as a planning body) at clearly defined intersections of the delivery process. Furthermore, the law should establish the regulator's role to approve proposed infrastructure investment, including generation and transmission.

Assuming an initial lack of expert staff, the regulator should initially focus on maintaining the integrity of the planning process. Over time, the regulator can learn to identify the key aspects (methodologies, tools, and data), that would benefit from an in-depth review of subject matter details using in-house capabilities (e.g., demand forecasting, technology evaluation, risk management). The initial focus in the set-up of the regulatory body will be to ensure that all relevant laws, regulations, and policy targets are being followed. It is pertinent that PLN, as central planner, follows the main principles for good planning and that all stakeholders in the plan are provided the opportunity to contribute to the final results. The regulator will not judge on the outcome of the RUPTL, but on whether or not the planning process was sound. With advancing expertise, after two cycles, the regulator should be able to review and approve proposed project proposals by itself.

To perform the regulatory tasks necessary to enhance the RUPTL, we propose to establish a planning board with 15 to 20 expert board members, consisting of one head of board, a small group of lawyers, a medium-sized group of energy and electricity scenario developers (economists, energy and electricity analysts, modelers with forecasting and risk identification experience), in addition to a larger group of technical staff capable of scrutinizing and understanding investment proposals, planning tools, and new technical concepts.

Section 3 also proposes the regulator to review tariff proposals and associated costs for transmission and generation infrastructure, as well as (in the long run) to approve tariff setting while protecting the poor. The existing legal foundation from the 2009 Electricity Law has to be critically reviewed and potentially updated to reflect the new regulatory roles. It will be important to empower the regulator to collect all relevant data to establish calculation methodologies and parameters (where necessary) and decide upon costs and tariffs for customer groups. To perform the regulatory tasks associated with enhancing the RUPTL, we propose establishing a planning board with 10 to 12 expert board members. Tariff setting decisions require legal, economic, accounting, and social expertise. The majority of the staff is likely to focus on applying data-driven assessment models and statistical tools. However, the staff must include numerous social experts who can support the determination of the threshold needed to protect the poor and the associated redistribution of burdens among customer groups. It is also crucial to include a smaller group of lawyers in the staff to ensure decisions are made in line with legal requirements.

Any decisions related to staffing involved in technical decision-making, starting from board members upwards, will have to be taken with great care. It is clear that building in-house staff competency takes time and strategic education. The body must also have the ability to retain experts. While the abovementioned framework will allow experts to develop and become decision-makers in order for third parties to understand the decisions being made, the framework cannot fully protect against vested interests. Relying on staff associated with certain groups of institutions such as PLN or the political sphere can raise doubts as to the integrity of the regulatory body's decisions. One way to minimize or avoid reliance on a certain group of experts can be to initially rely more heavily on outside expertise (e.g. consultancy firms), and, if impossible otherwise, select staff with experience from inside certain institutions that do not have any further ties to former employers.

At the same time, the head of the regulatory agency can and potentially should be a former senior industry representative or government figure, who will be respected and has experience with influencing decision-makers from politics and the industry.

Market Design

Transformation of the electricity sector structure in Indonesia needs to be assessed in the context of the current state control provisions. It is beyond the scope of this report to evaluate the legal framework in Indonesia and its impact on any electricity market restructuring initiative. Without the intention to indicate preferences or to recommend a specific structure, this section briefly introduces, at a high level, the additional role for electricity regulatory bodies if unbundling is enacted.

The general electricity market structure has implications on the required regulatory scope and depth of actions. Over the past 40 years, the primary focus of public policy in the electricity industry was to establish positive, practical experience to gain competencies in the competitive provisions and use of generation infrastructure as one segment of the electricity industry. Chile (early 1980s) is widely regarded as the frontrunner in this context, introducing vertical and horizontal unbundling of generation, transmission, and distribution, as well as full privatization of all these functions. Through horizontal unbundling, the assets of the former state-owned company Endesa were privatized and allocated to an overall 14 different companies, including 6 main generation, 6 main distribution, and 2 isolated generation and distribution companies. Vertical unbundling has led to the formation of stand-alone companies that solely provide transmission services to all relevant market participants. During times of deep market reform, the UK (from 1989 onwards), several states in North America (from early 1990s onwards), and in Continental Europe (from 1996 onwards) all introduced various forms of unbundling in their respective electricity industries, as well as competition into the generation function. In almost all cases, with Argentina being the rare exemption (and only for a short time), the transmission function was (and still is) considered a natural monopoly. These electricity market structures all rely on economic regulation to ensure that network service companies mimic competitive decision-making. At the same time, competition in the generation segment allowed for individual decision-making for time, location, volume, technology, and price of investments.

Not all cases aimed at the privatization of state-owned assets, and a significant share of public ownership remain in several of the electricity markets with applied unbundling.

Governments aim to achieve a diverse set of objectives through the introduction of unbundling. Often, horizontal unbundling is implemented to allow several generation asset owners to compete for customers and to spread investment and operational risks in the generation function across various owners. At the same time, vertical unbundling is introduced to achieve transparency on matters such as financial management and accounting of costs in all functions of the electricity industry. This transparency is a cornerstone for achieving good governance in the electricity industry.

In the context of European electricity sector legislation packages (1996, 2003, 2009), vertical unbundling became increasingly regarded as a decisive factor to make competition between generators work. Curbing the powers of vertically integrated utilities, who own both transmission and generation assets, has reduced the ability of these entities that own the transmission market to discriminate competitors through controlling generation function, transmission access, and/or through fixing unfair pricing strategies.

In the context of countries or states without (full) competition in the generation function, transmission unbundling of accounts is still widely used. The resulting separation between segments allows regulatory bodies to plan and approve transmission expansion, approve transmission tariffs, and ensure open transmission access (for example, to IPPs). There remain many states in the US where vertically integrated utility companies exist in addition to a public utility commission. This commission is responsible for monitoring and enforcing open access rules and long-term planning approaches. The same set up is applied in countries such as South Africa and Nigeria, and countries from regions such as Central and Latin America. The application of unbundling indicates the general relevance for the electricity industry, almost independent of additional structures in the industry.

European countries have predominately favored transmission system operators under ownership unbundling, but also other unbundling systems have been established. According to the Council of European Energy Regulators (CEER, 2016), 70% of all transmission system operators (TSO) in Europe are ownership unbundled, 12% apply an independent transmission operator model, and 6% apply an independent system operator model (ISO). This contrasts the ISO model in other parts of the world, notably in the US, where around two-thirds of all electricity supplied is administered through an ISO, Australia, Scotland, and Latin American countries.

Certification is the main regulatory task in managing unbundling, independent of the unbundling structure. Commonly, certification procedures are used to ensure that transmission-owning companies comply with unbundling provisions to ensure that transmission, generation, and supply are independent from each other. Certification is often initially completed at the time the transmission company signals the intention to commence operations, and penalties may be applied. In most cases, the regulatory bodies are responsible for the certification process, with the government approving the outcome and designating the transmission company. Europe has seen the emergence of unbundling compliance officers within companies and schemes that put the burden of proof on the transmission owner and not the regulatory body. The most prominent violations of unbundling provisions that have been noted in the past 20 years include unclear exercise of control and rights in the company; low level of resources to maintain the functions of the company; unclear definition of the company's tasks; lack of independent management and board members, including issue of conflict of interest at end of their terms; and the lack of separation between ministries and transmission companies. In some of the situations noted above, penalties and sanctions have been applied. In some circumstances, companies have been notified about the possibility to re-open the certification process and, in few cases, certifications have been revoked.

As observed in countries and states with applied unbundling structures, an unbundling model with less structural changes compared to ownership unbundling, e.g., unbundling of accounts and legal unbundling, will require a strong regulatory body that has the means to detect and enforce discriminatory practices from vertically integrated companies. Furthermore, unbundling alone is not sufficient to attract more investment into the industry; this action has to be complemented by further frameworks in case of inadequate investment patterns.

A fundamental difference between the European TSO model (mostly with ownership unbundling) and the ISO model is the asset ownership of the transmission infrastructure. The ISO model separates the operational functions from other companies in the industry and does not allow the network operator to own the transmission assets. As such, the primary focus of the ISO is to ensure the system operates and is dispatched in accordance with the established conditions (often: security-constrained, least-cost, economic dispatch). The European TSO model may rely more heavily on transmission infrastructure build-out (as opposed to operational or technological alternatives) and may require more in-depth regulatory approaches. However, there is no evidence for a clear winning TSO arrangement yet (Chawla and Pollitt 2014).

Appendix 1:
How Other Sectors in Indonesia Have Implemented Regulators

As mentioned in this report, the 2002 Electricity Law once introduced a regulatory body in the electricity sector, the Electricity Market Supervisory Agency (BPPTL). BPPTL is a government agency that has the authority and responsibility to make independent decisions pertaining to electricity regulations, including supervising electricity supply in areas that are open to competition. There are also various regulatory bodies in different sectors such as

   a.   Indonesian Toll Road Authority (BPJT) in the highway and toll road sector;

   b.   Statistics Indonesia (BPS) in the statistics sector;

   c.   Indonesian Telecommunication Regulatory Body (BRTI);

   d.   Oil and Gas Upstream Business Activities Operational Agency (BP Migas), Temporary Working Operational Unit (SKS). and Special Task Force for Upstream Oil and Gas Business Activities (SKK Migas) in the oil and gas sector; and

   e.   Overseas Commercial Loan Management Coordination Team (PKLN).

The following tables provides a comparison of the regulatory bodies in Indonesia.

Table A1: Comparison of Regulatory Body in Indonesia

No.	Identification	Electricity	Oil and Gas		Toll Road	Statistic	Telecommunication	Financing
		BPPTL	BP Migas	SKK Migas	BPJT	BPS	BRTI	PKLN
1.	Legal Basis	2002 Electricity Law as further regulated under Government Regulation No. 53 of 2003 on BPPTL (GR 53/2003).	Oil and Gas Law, dissolved through MK Decision 36 and replaced by the Temporary Working Operational Unit (SKS) through MEMR Decree 3135/2012 and MEMR Decree 3136/2012.	Presidential Regulation No. 9 of 2013 on the Management of Upstream Oil and Gas Activities as amended by PR 36/2018 (PR 9/2013) established SKK Migas to replace SKS.	Law No. 38 of 2004 on Road (Law 38/2004) and further regulated under Government Regulation No. 15 of 2005 on Toll Road; and established through MOPWH Regulation No. 295/PRT/M/2005.	Law No. 6 of 1960 on Census and Law No. 7 of 1960 on Statistics formed the Central Bureau of Statistics. The Central Bureau of Statistics was renamed to BPS by Presidential Regulation No. 86 of 2007 on BPS (PR 86/2007).	Law No. 36 of 1999 on Telecommunication (Law 36/1999) and further regulated under the Decree of Minister of Communication 31 of 2003 on Determination of Indonesian Telecommunication Regulatory Body as last amended by Regulation of MOCI No. 15 of 2018 on BRTI.	Presidential Decree No. 39 of 1991 on Overseas Commercial Loan Management Coordination (PD 39/1991).
2.	Appointment and Accountability	The head of BPPTL and members of BPPTL are appointed by the President with the approval of DPR. BPPTL is an independent body authorized to make decisions without influence from other parts of the government.	The head of BP Migas is appointed and terminated by the President through a MEMR Decree. after consulting with the DPR and in carrying out the duties, the head of BP Migas shall be responsible to the President.	The head of SKK Migas, after getting consideration from the Supervisory Commission, is appointed and terminated by the President through a Presidential Decree, as proposed by the MEMR. The head of SKK is directly responsible to the President.	The head and board members of BPJT are appointed and dissolved by MOPWH through MOPWH Decree. BPJT works under and is accountable to the MOPWH.	The head of BPS, Main Secretariat, deputy, and Main Inspectorate are appointed and dissolved by the President. While the other members of BPS (as mentioned below) are appointed and dissolved by the head of BPS; BPS is directly under and is responsible to the President on performing duties relating to statistics.	The members of BRTI are appointed through MOCI Decree. BRTI works under and is responsible to the MOCI.	PKLN is appointed through Presidential Decree and is responsible to the President.

continued on next page

Table A1:   *continued*

3.	Organization Structure	BPPTL is led by a head and odd-numbered board members of at least 5 people and at most 11 people.	BP Migas is comprised of a management board, in addition to expert, technical, and administrative staff.	SKK Migas board members are comprised of (i) a head; (ii) a vice head; (iii) a secretary; (iv) an internal supervisor; and (vi) deputies, for a maximum of 5 people.	BPJT board members are comprised of 3 groups of representatives: (i) 3 members from government bureaucracy; (ii) 1 from the academic community or civil society; and (iii) 1 from a related expert or professional association and civil society. The members are chosen to fulfill the participation element of good governance promotion.	BPS is led by the head and its members are comprised of (i) a Main Secretariat, (ii) a deputy of Methodology and Statistical Information, (iii) a deputy of Social Statistics, (iv) a deputy of Production Statistics, (v) a deputy of Distribution and Services of Statistics, (vi) a deputy of Balance Sheet and Statistic Analysis, (vii) a Main Inspectorate, (viii) members of an Education and Training Center, and (ix) a vertical agency.	BRTI is comprised of (i) a directorate general of Postal and Telecommunication or a directorate general of Resources and Devices of Postal and Information Technology; (ii) a directorate general of Information Applications; and (iii) a Committee of Telecommunication Regulations (consisting of both government and community elements).	PKLN is led by the coordinating minister of Economy, Finance, Industry and Development Supervision. PKLN members are comprised of (i) a minister/ secretary of state, (ii) a minister of Finance, (iii) a state minister of National Development Planning/ head of the National Development Planning Agency, (iv) a minister of Industry, (v) a state minister of Research and Technology/chair of BPP Technology; (vi) a minister of Transportation, (vii) a minister of Tourism, Post and Telecommunications, (viii) a minister of Mining and Energy, (ix) a minister of Public Works, (x) a governor of the Bank Indonesia.

continued on next page

Table A1:   *continued*

No.	Identification	Electricity	Oil and Gas		Toll Road	Statistic	Telecommunication	Financing
		BPPTL	BP Migas	SKK Migas	BPJT	BPS	BRTI	PKLN
4.	Function	Regulate and supervise electricity supply business in areas of the electricity sector that are open to competition.	Supervise upstream business activities to ensure that the exploitation of oil and gas that is state owned is utilized to give the maximum benefit and revenue to the state for the maximum prosperity of the people.	Same as BP Migas	Manage the government's authority in the operation of toll road including regulation, concession and monitoring to ensure the maximum benefit to the country and public welfare.	(i) Review, compile, and formulate policies in the field of statistics. (ii) Coordinate national and regional statistics activities. (iii) Stipulate and implement basic statistics. (iv) Establish a national statistics system. (v) Foster and facilitate the activities of government agencies in the field of statistical activities. (vi) Organize fostering and general administrative services in the field of general planning, organization, governance, staffing, finance, filing, public relations, law, equipment, and household.	Regulate, supervise, and control the transparency, independence, accountability, and fairness principle in regulation, supervision, and control of information and communication technology.	Coordinate the management of foreign commercial loans.

continued on next page

Table A1: *continued*

5.	Duties					

	a. Elaborate and apply the government's general policies.
	b. Prevent unfair business competition.
	c. Regulate the selling price of electricity, the cost of providing facilities, transmission infrastructure rent and the rental price of electricity distribution.
	d. Monitor and supervise the implementation of provisions concerning levies on transmission facilities and electricity distribution facilities.
	e. Supervise the selling price of electricity at the competed side of the electricity generation and sales agent business.
	f. Regulate and supervise the business of electricity market managers and electric power system managers by
		The function and duties of SKK Migas are essentially the same as BP Migas.
		
		a. Advise the MEMR on policy for the preparation and offer of a work area and PSC.
		b. Sign a PSC.
		c. Assess and submit the development plan for the first field to be operated in a work area to the MEMR for approval.
		d. Approve field development plans other than that as referred to in letter c.
		e. Approve work programs and budget.
		f. Monitor and report to the MEMR on the implementation of the cooperation contact.
		g. Appoint the seller of crude oil and/or natural gas to the government that gives the maximum benefit to the state.
			Perform government tasks in the field of statistics.
			
			a. Recommend initial tariff and toll tariff adjustment to MOPWH.
			b. Conduct acquisition of rights to toll road concessions and recommend the subsequent operation to the MOPWH.
			c. If required, temporarily acquiesce failed toll road concession rights, and re-auction these rights in the future.
			d. Conduct preparation for the toll road concession, including analyzing the financial feasibility, feasibility study, and AMDAL preparation.
				a. Draft and stipulate regulations on
				  i. Telecommunications: standard operating performance, standards of service quality and telecommunication tools and equipment, interconnection fees, development of broadcasting digitalization and multimedia; and arrangement of radio frequency spectrum and satellite orbit.
				  ii. Informatics: improvement of technology and infrastructure of informatics, informatics empowerment, digital economics and internet;
				b. supervise (i) operation performance, business competition, utilization of telecommunication tools and equipment and radio frequency spectrum and satellite orbit; and (ii) improvement of technology and infrastructure of informatics, informatics empowerment, digital economics and internet;
					i. Coordinate the management of all foreign commercial loans.
					ii. Determine the total amount of foreign commercial loans to be borrowed from international capital markets in a fiscal year and establish guidelines on the terms of foreign commercial loans.
					iii. Establish the priority of foreign commercial loans.
					iv. Establish the order of time for loan search in the international capital market.
					v. Establish ways and procedures for applying for approval to seek foreign commercial loans as well as methods and procedures for periodic reporting
					vi. Monitor plans and implementation and use of foreign commercial loans.

continued on next page

Table A1:   *continued*

No.	Identification	Electricity	Oil and Gas		Toll Road	Statistic	Telecommunication	Financing
		BPPTL	BP Migas	SKK Migas	BPJT	BPS	BRTI	PKLN
		i. determining the area of distribution and business of electric power sales, ii. issuing IUPTLs for each type of UPTL, and iii. ensuring that the provisions of the legislation and the provisions of the permit are compiled by the IUPTL holders.					c. control (i) settlement of disputes between telecommunication network operators and services providers, implementation of service quality standards, utilization of telecommunication tools and equipment and radio frequency spectrum and satellite orbit; and (ii) implement improvement of technology and infrastructure of informatics, informatics empowerment, digital economics and internet.	vii. Take necessary steps to ensure the coordination of the management of foreign commercial loans is well carried out and reaches intended targets.

continued on next page

Table A1:   *continued*

g. Conduct hearings with the public and establish rules.

h. Facilitate the settlement of disputes.

i. Apply administrative sanctions to holders of IUPTL for violations.

j. Guarantee electricity supply.

AMDAL = analisis mengenai dampak lingkungan (environmental impact analysis), BP Migas = Badan Pelaksana Kegiatan Usaha Hulu Minyak dan Gas Bumi (Oil and Gas Upstream Business Activities Operational Agency), BPPTL = Badan Pengawas Pasar Tenaga Listrik (Electricity Market Supervisory Agency), BPS = Badan Pusat Statistik (Statistics Indonesia), BPP Technology = Badan Pengkajian dan Penerapan Teknologi (Agency for the Assessment and Application of Technology), BRTI = Badan Regulasi Telekomunikasi Indonesia (Indonesian Telecommunication Regulatory Body), GR = government regulation, IUPTL = izin usaha penyediaan tenaga listrik (electricity supply business permit), MEMR = Kementerian Energi dan Sumber Daya Mineral (Ministry of Energy and Mineral Resources), MK = Mahkamah Konstitusi (Constitutional Court), MOCI = Kementerian Komunikasi dan Informatika (Ministry of Communication and Informatics), MOPWH = Kementerian Pekerjaan Umum dan Perumahan Rakyat (Ministry of Public Works and Housing), PD = presidential decree, PKLN = pengelolaan pinjaman komersial luar negeri (overseas commercial loan management coordination), PSC = production sharing contract, SKK Migas = Satuan Kerja Khusus Pelaksana Kegiatan Usaha Hulu Minyak dan Gas Bumi (Special Task Force for Upstream Oil and Gas Business Activities), SKS = satuan kerja sementara (temporary working operational unit), UPTL = electricity supply business.

Source: Authors, based on the following: Government Regulation No. 53/2003 on BPPTL; MEMR Decree No. 3135/2012 and MEMR Decree No. 3136/2012 on Temporary Working Operational Unit; Presidential Regulation No. 36/2018 on the Management of Upstream Oil and Gas Activities which established SKK Migas; Law No. 38 of 2004 on Road; Government Regulation No. 15 of 2005 on Toll Road; MOPWH Regulation No. 295/PRT/M/2005; Law No. 6 of 1960 on Census; Law No. 7 of 1960 on Statistics; Presidential Regulation No. 86 of 2007 on BPS; Law No. 36 of 1999 on Telecommunication; Minister of Communication Decree No. 31 of 2003 on Determination of Indonesian Telecommunication Regulatory Body as last amended by Regulation of MOCI No. 15 of 2018; and Presidential Decree No. 39 of 1991 on Overseas Commercial Loan Management Coordination.

Appendix 2:
The Stakeholders

As briefly mentioned in the overview of the regulatory framework on the electricity sector in Indonesia, its stakeholders are as follows:

1. Ministry of Mineral and Energy Resources

    The Ministry of Mineral and Energy Resources (MEMR) is responsible for creating and implementing Indonesia's energy policy, including the production of the National Electricity Plan. The MEMR is also authorized to regulate the power sector through the Directorate General of Electricity and the Directorate General of New and Renewable Energy and Energy Conservation.

2. House of Representatives

    The House of Representatives (DPR) is a legislative body in Indonesia. Particularly, Commission VII of the DPR is responsible for the development of regulations in the areas of energy, research, technology, and the environment. Thus, Commission VIII is responsible for the approval of energy-related legislation, including electricity and the supervision of government policies related to energy.

3. State-Owned Electricity Company

    The State-Owned Electricity Company (PLN) is responsible for most of Indonesia's power generation, and has exclusive power over the transmission, distribution, and supply of electricity to the public. PLN is supervised by the MEMR, the Ministry of State-Owned Enterprises, and the Ministry of Finance (MOF). The 2009 Electricity Law removed PLN's role as the authorized holder of the only electricity business license under the previous Electricity Law issued in 1985. PLN is now simply the holder of an electricity supply business permit. The 2009 Electricity Law grants the right of first refusal to PLN for the supply of electricity in an area before the central government or regional governments can offer such right to regional-owned entities, private entities, cooperatives, or self-reliant community institutions.[1]

4. National Development Planning Agency

    The National Development Planning Agency (BAPPENAS) is responsible for carrying out government duties in the field of national development planning in accordance with the prevailing laws and regulations. Within BAPPENAS is the Directorate for Public–Private Partnership which facilitates cooperation on infrastructure projects between the government and private investors, including electricity infrastructure.[2]

---

[1] Government of Indonesia. 2009. *Law No. 30 concerning Electricity, Article 11 (2)*. Jakarta.
[2] Capital Investment Coordinating Board (BKPM). **Main Duty and Functions**.

5. Investment Coordinating Board

    The Investment Coordinating Board (BKPM) is the authority responsible for issuing business licenses, including IUPTL for electricity supply business activities. It acts as a "one-stop-shop" integrated service for business start-up and licensing procedures, as well as for facilitating foreign workers' permits. BKPM also offers an Investor Relations Unit to provide information on and deal with enquiries from existing and potential investors.[3] However, after the issuance of Government Regulation No. 24/ 2018 on Online Single Submission Services, most licensing documents are now processed through this online system based on the process described in Government Regulation No. 24/ 2018. There are still several licenses which were previously handled by BKPM that are excluded from Government Regulation No. 24/ 2018and therefore must still be processed via BKPM's system, where the list of these licenses can be seen under Article 4(2) of Head of BKPM Regulation No. 6/2018 on Guidelines and Procedures for the Implementation of Capital Investment Licensing and Facilities. Currently, BKPM is the only body authorized by the government to act as the Online Single Submission Agency.

6. Committee for the Acceleration of Prioritized Infrastructure Development

    The Committee for the Acceleration of Prioritized Infrastructure Development (KPPIP) is an inter-ministerial coordinating committee chaired by the Coordinating Ministry for Economic Affairs (CMEA) with the Coordinating Ministry of Maritime Affairs as the vice chair. Other members of KPPIP include the MOF, BAPPENAS, Ministry of Agrarian and Spatial Planning, and the Ministry of Environment and Forestry. KPPIP was established with the main objective of coordinating the decision-making process. KPPIP is the main point of contact for expediting national and strategically important projects.[4]

    As stipulated in Presidential Regulation No. 75/2014 on Acceleration of Priority Infrastructure as amended by Presidential Regulation No. 122/2016, the CMEA, as the chair of KPPIP, is given the authority to form a sector work team and an inter-sector work team when required. In its implementation, the work team for the program Acceleration of Electricity Infrastructure Delivery was established by a virtue of the CMEA Decree No. 129 of 2015 on Working Team in Acceleration of Infrastructure Provision on Electricity. The legal basis for founding the Implementation Unit for National Electricity Development Program was established through this decree.[5]

7. Ministry of Finance

    The MOF approves tax incentives that may be offered by the government for a power project, as well as any government guarantees. The Directorate of Government Support Management and Infrastructure Financing within the MOF is responsible for reviewing guarantee requests. Any approved guarantee is administered by the Indonesian Infrastructure Guarantee Fund (IIGF).

    Additionally, the MOF recommends the maximum electricity subsidy to PLN in the national budget and reviews loan arrangements entered into by PLN. This review includes the government guarantees for PLN's loans.

8. Ministry of State-Owned Enterprises

    The Ministry of State-Owned Enterprises supervises PLN's management as a state-owned enterprise (SOE), sets its corporate performance targets, and approves its annual budget and asses the achievement of those targets.

---

[3] Footnote 2
[4] The Committee for the Acceleration of Prioritized Infrastructure Development (KPPIP). Composition and Organizational Structure.
[5] Footnote 4.

9. The Indonesia Infrastructure Guarantee Fund

    The IIGF was established on 30 December 2009 to provide guarantees for infrastructure projects. The IIGF also acts as a strategic advisor to the government and a transaction manager and lead arranger for infrastructure projects. The IIGF is wholly owned by the government, with IDR6 trillion in capital injected as at the end of 2015. The government injected an additional IDR1 trillion the following year.[6]

    In August 2018, to support electricity infrastructure, the MOF issued MOF Regulation No. 101/PMK.08/2018 on "Procedures for the Provision and Implementation of Government Guarantee Jointly or Through Indonesia Infrastructure Guarantee Corporation Against Default Risk of SOE Obtaining Loans and/or Issuing Bonds for Financing the Provision of Infrastructure."

10. PT Sarana Multi Infrastruktur

    PT Sarana Multi Infrastruktur (PT SMI) is an infrastructure financing company which was established on 26 February 2009 as an SOE to have 100% shares owned by the Government of Indonesia through its minister of finance.

    PT SMI plays an active role in facilitating infrastructure financing as well as preparing projects and providing advisory services for infrastructure projects in Indonesia. PT SMI's responsibilities include supporting the government's infrastructure development agenda for Indonesia through partnerships with private and/or multilateral financial institutions, known as public–private partnership projects. As such, PT SMI can serve as a catalyst in accelerating infrastructure development in Indonesia. The electricity sector can be financed by PT SMI.[7]

---

[6]   Indonesia Infrastructure Guarantee Fund. **Company History and Milestones.**
[7]   PT Sarana Multi Infrastruktur. **About Us.**

Appendix 3:
Timeline of Regulatory Framework
for Indonesia Electricity

1985 Electricity Law

Early electricity arrangements in Indonesia were carried out pursuant to the 1890 Dutch Ordinance titled "Installation and Utilization of Conductors for Electrical Lighting and Transferring Power via Electricity in Indonesia."[8] This ordinance was annulled in 1985 with the introduction of the 1985 Electricity Law, which ushered in the modern era of the power sector in Indonesia.[9] The 1985 Electricity Law established a centralized system with the State-Owned Electricity Company (PLN) holding exclusive powers over the transmission, distribution and sale of electricity.[10]

Under the 1985 Electricity Law, private participation in power generation was limited to an entity's own use or for sale to PLN. Essentially, the model allowed for private investment in power generating assets only as an independent power producer licensed to sell their power solely to PLN, pursuant to a power purchase agreement.

Financing of the Paiton Thermal Power Project in 1989 marked the beginning of the end of the World Bank's special relationship with the Indonesian government in the power sector, in large part because it coincided with the advent of Indonesia's experiment with private participation in the sector.[11] Several other significant independent power producers followed thereafter.

2002 Electricity Law: The Distinction Between Competitive and Noncompetitive Areas

i) Electricity supply business in areas where competition applies:

The stipulation of a competition area will be determined in stages based on the level of readiness of the electricity supply business. The area readiness is evaluated on the criteria of the sufficiency of power reserves, transmission networks, and extensive distribution networks. This determination will also include consideration of the costs that may arise as a result of changes in government policies. All electricity supply business activities in the areas where competition applies can be conducted if such business entity obtains the necessary electricity supply business permit (IUPTL) issued by the Electricity Market Supervisory Agency (BPPTL). Article 16 unbundled electricity provisions on businesses, meaning that the scope of IUPTLs as stipulated in Article 8 (2) shall be handled separately by a different business entity. It is because the government saw that for the implementation of fair and healthy competition, electricity supply businesses (which consisted of seven divisions) need to be carried out separately by different business entities.

---

[8]   MT Sambodo. 2016. *From Darkness to Light*. Singapore: ISEAS Publishing.
[9]   Refer to footnote 1 for more infomation.
[10]   Government of Indonesia. 1985. *Electricity Law, Article 7*. Jakarta.
[11]   F. Seymour and A. Sari. 2002. Indonesia: Electricity Reform under Economic Crisis. In N. Dubash, ed. *Power Politics, Equity and Environment in Electricity Reform*. Washington, DC: World Resources Institute.

Article 17 promoted competition, and a prohibition on monopolies and unfair competition. Specifically, it was stipulated that that business entities in the field of electricity generation in one area of competition are prohibited from dominating the market. One area of competition here is defined as an area determined by the government as an area open to competition. Establishing a competition area includes consideration of, but not limited to, generating capacity, level of electricity demand, readiness of interconnection systems, and socioeconomic aspects.

However, competition in this case was not applicable for transmission and distribution (T&D), of which the SOE is given the priority right. The competition for T&D was not applicable because T&D has the characteristics of a natural monopoly and therefore must be regulated by BPPTL. However, in conducting T&D, the SOEs may cooperate with other business entities if such SOEs were not able to make the necessary investment. However, there was still equal access for electricity transmission that was integrated into the national transmission network for all electricity generation providers, while operators of distribution facilities were obliged to provide equal access to the electricity sales business and electricity sales agent (ESA).

Holders of IUPTL were prohibited from conducting business mergers in interconnected networks in areas where competition applies, as this could have resulted in market domination and unfair business competition. However, exceptions could be made if they approved by BPPTL.

Furthermore, the 2002 Electricity Law also regulated some provisions on the electricity selling price in areas where competition applies. Pursuant to Article 21 (3), electricity shall be sold through an ESA to customers that are connected to middle and high-voltage grid networks, where the selling price is based on reasonable and fair competition under the supervision of the BPPTL. Meanwhile, for customers that were connected to the low-voltage grid, electricity shall be sold by an electricity sales business where the selling price shall be determined by BPPTL. Therefore, the 2002 Electricity Law opened market mechanisms for the determination of electricity tariff in a competition area. However, an ESA may sell the electricity to the consumer that is connected to a low-voltage grid with a prior permission from BPPTL. The consideration in granting licenses to ESAs to serve low-voltage consumers is based on the demand of low-voltage consumers to obtain better electricity quality and special services.

The Exception

If the operation of business activities such as electricity transmission, electricity market management, and electric power systems management were not technically ready yet, considering their vital roles, such types of business can be carried out jointly by the SOEs.

ii) Electricity supply business in an area that is not or not yet a competitive market

The 2002 Electricity Law contained provisions for introducing market competition, vertically unbundling the industry, and encouraging enhanced private sector participation. However, under Article 30, in an area that is not or not yet applying competition due to certain conditions relating to geographic and/or socioeconomic factors, the electricity supply business can be integrated in a vertical ownership of electricity supply facilities ranging from electricity generation to the electricity sales to consumers. Such electricity supply businesses will be prioritized to the SOE that has been assigned by the government to carry out the electricity supply in the area which is not or not yet applying a competition.

Contrary to areas where competition applies in which the electricity price will be determined by BPPTL, in an area which is not or not yet applying a competition, the selling price will be determined by the government or regional government.

Table A3.1 describing the essential provisions under the 2002 Electricity Law:

Table A3.1:   Main Provisions of the 2002 Electricity Law

Items	Electricity Supply Business in an Area Where Competition Applies	Electricity Supply Business in an Area Which is Not or Not Yet Applying a Competition
Bundling/Unbundling Concept	Article 16 unbundled the electricity provision on businesses, which means that the scope of an electricity supply business under Article 8 (2) below shall be handled separately by a different business entity as follows: i. electricity generation (a consumer that is connected to middle and high-voltage grid can purchase electricity on a bilateral basis from other generation that does not enter the electricity market); ii. electricity transmission; iii. electricity distribution; iv. electricity sales business; v. electricity sales agent where the selling business is conducted to the low voltage grid customers; vi. electricity market manager; and vii. electricity system manager.	Article 30 provides alternative choices for electricity supply businesses under Article 8 (2) whether it will be conducted in bundled/integrated or unbundled manner.
SOEs Priority	A SOE is given the first priority to conduct T&D where the competition is not applicable	A SOE is given the first priority to conduct the scope of Electricity Supply Business
Selling Prices Mechanism	Electricity shall be sold by the ESA to customers that are connected to middle and high-voltage grid networks, where the selling price shall be based on reasonable and fair competition which will be under the supervision of BPPTL. For costumers that are connected to low-voltage grids, electricity shall be sold by an electricity sales business where the selling price shall be determined by BPPTL.	Contrary to areas where competition applies in which the electricity price will be determined by BPPTL, in an area which is not or not yet a competitive market, the selling price will be determined by the government or regional government

BPPTL = Badan Pengawas Pasar Tenaga Listrik (Electricity Market Supervisory Agency), ESA = electricity sales agent, SOE = state-owned enterprise, T&D = transmission and distribution.

Source: Authors, based on analysis of the 2002 Electricity Law.

Decision 001

The 2002 Electricity Law was annulled by the Constitutional Court (MK) on 21 December 2004 through Decision 001 as the concept of unbundling the system in the 2002 Electricity Law was deemed to contradict Article 33 of the 1945 Constitution paragraphs (1), (2), (3), and (4) along with the statement that the state has the right to control land, water, and any resources therein, including electricity, in order to meet the needs of the greater people. The following table on summary of Decision 001.

Appendix 3

Table A3.2:   Summary of MK Decision 001

No.	Article	Petitioner's Arguments	MK Consideration	MK Decision
1.	Article 1 (18) Electricity supply business license (IUPTL) is a license to conduct business of electricity supply for public interest.	• The fact that supply of electricity is conducted based on a competitive system is contradictory to the spirit of IUPTL. The petitioner argued that while electricity supply business activity must be done for public interest, the nature of business actor will always be profit-oriented.[a]	• The meaning of state control in this context should be construed as the state's authority to issue IUPTL for business actors.[b]	MK did not decide on this petition.
2.	Article 15 (2) Conditions for determining business areas that can apply competition of electricity as referred to in paragraph (1) include a. the selling price level of electricity that has reached its economy; b. competition for primary energy supply; c. Electricity Market Supervisory Agency (BPPTL) has been formed; d. readiness of the rules needed in the application of competition; e. readiness of infrastructure, hardware, and software of electricity system(s); f. conditions of system(s) that make it possible to have competition; g. equality of business entities that will compete; and h. other conditions as stipulated by the decree of the Leader of BPPTL.	• This article demonstrates that there is no consideration on the socioeconomic conditions of the people to purchase electricity.[c] • The existence of such business area(s) will create problems in the people's ability to afford electricity.[d]	• The conditions to determine tariff under Article 15 (2) is not in line with the actual socioeconomic conditions of the people, thus, it is contradictory to Article 33 (2) of the Indonesian Constitution.[e] • It should be highlighted that the state's authority to control tariff stipulation should be in the form of drafting regulation on the calculation of tariff using the approach of cost recovery and sales tariffs for certain categories of people (rural area and/or in poverty).[f]	MK granted the claims related to the conditions to determine if a market is to be a competitive market. MK did not agree that existence of such business areas will create problems in the people's ability to afford electricity priced because the price of electricity is still controlled by the state through regulation.

BPPTL = Badan Pengawas Pasar Tenaga Listrik (Electricity Market Supervisory Agency), IUPTL = Izin Usaha Penyediaan Tenaga Listrik (Electricity Supply Business Permit), MK = Mahkamah Konstitusi (Constitutional Court).
[a] Government of Indonesia, Constitutional Court. 2003. *Decision No. 001-021-022/PUU-I/2003*. Jakarta. p. 40, point 4.4.6.
[b] Footnote a, p. 197.
[c] Footnote a, p. 126.
[d] Footnote a, p. 126.
[e] Footnote a, p. 133, point 4.
[f] Footnote a, p. 47, point 4.

Source: Asian Development Bank.

Decision 149

Similar to the argument raised in Decision 001, PLN's labor union also challenged the unbundling concept under the 2009 Electricity Law. In the Decision 149, MK rejected the petitioner's requests in its entirety.[12] Even though MK referred to and highlighted the former Decision 001, Decision 149 came up with a completely different treatment of the unbundling concept.

In its decision, MK allows the unbundling concept under the 2009 Electricity Law based on MK's interpretation of Decision 001, which can be summed up as follows:[13] (i) the government as the majority shareholder (of PLN), still exercises its control on the decision-making level; (ii) Article 33 of the Indonesian Constitution does not prohibit privatization, as long as such privatization does not eliminate the control of the state; (iii) similarly Article 33 of the Indonesian Constitution does not prohibit competition among the providers either as long as such competition does not eliminate the control of the state including the control to govern, to manage, and to supervise existing important branches of production for the greatest benefit of the people; and (iv) emphasizing the unbundling concept implemented by various companies under Article 16 of 2002 Electricity Law will only lead to the deterioration of PLN and the nonsustainability of electricity supply to the people.[14]

There is an inconsistency between the former Decision 001 and the latter Decision 149 in the context of the unbundling concept in the electricity sector. In Decision 001, it was strictly stipulated that electricity was considered a public utility that falls under the category of "existing important branches of production" and it should therefore be controlled by the state. In contrast, Decision 149 interprets Article 33 of the Indonesian Constitution to be more flexible. Decision 149 states that Article 33 does not prohibit unbundling and competition in the electricity sector because the unbundling concept in the 2009 Electricity Law is different than the one in the 2002 Electricity Law. This, however, still constitutes the separation of the electricity industry and generally falls under the same concept of unbundling. MK also clearly stipulates that it is sufficient for the government to exercise control over electricity without having to own the commodity itself. The following table on summary of Decision 149.

---

[12]   Constitutional Court of Republic of Indonesia, Decision 149, p.97.
[13]   Footnote 33, p. 91.
[14]   Refer to footnote 34 for more information.

Table A3.3:   **Summarizes Decision 149**

No.	Article	Petitioner's Arguments	MK Consideration	MK Decision
1.	**Article 10** 2. Electricity supply business for public purposes as referred to in paragraph (1) can be carried out in an integrated manner. 3. Electricity supply business for public purposes as referred to in paragraph (2) shall be carried out by one business entity in one business area. 4. The limitation of the business area as referred to in paragraph (3) also applies to electricity supply business(es) for public purposes which only covers the distribution of electricity and / or the sale of electricity.	• According to Article 33 (2) of the Indonesian Constitution, electricity, as one of the vital production sectors, affects the livelihood of the people and shall be controlled by the state; therefore, the limitation of business area in Article 10(3) and (4) of the 2009 Electricity Law are also limiting the state's control over electricity, which in this context should be unlimited.[a] • The separation of electricity business types will result in 1. vertical unbundling, which is the separation of electricity business supply based on the types of business supply (transmission, distribution, generation, and sales) which can be carried out by different companies; and 2. horizontal unbundling, which is the separation of electricity business supply based on the area of the electricity company, in which the operation of each state-owned entities, region-owned entities, and private entities must be in line with the criteria of an electricity business area.[c]	• Based on the previous Decision 001 regarding the judicial review of the 2002 Electricity Law, it can be concluded that Article 33 of the Indonesian Constitution does not prohibit privatization or competition between business actors, provided that such competition or privatization does not eliminate the state's control over the power to regulate, manage, organize, and supervise the electricity business sector as one of the vital production sectors for the state that can affect the livelihood of the people.[b] • Article 3 and Article 4 of the 2009 Electricity Law states that the state has the power to set the policy, regulation, supervision, and the implementation of the electricity supply business; therefore, these articles ensure that the state will not lose its control in the implementation of the electricity business supply.[d] • The provision in this article that states that electricity business supply can be carried out in an integrated manner is different than the previous unbundling provision contained in Article 16 of Law No. 20 of the 2002 on Electricity (2002 Electricity Law) clearly stated that electricity supply businesses shall be conducted separately by different business entities; therefore, this article is not an unbundling article since it does not eliminate the state's control in the electricity business supply, regardless of the separation of electricity types of business.[e]	MK rejected all requests of the petitioners.

continued on next page

Table A3.3:   *continued*

2.	Article 11		
	3. For regions that have not received electricity service, the government or regional government, in accordance with their authorities, gives opportunity to region-owned enterprises, private business entities, or cooperatives to be providers of integrated electricity supply businesses.	• The petitioners argue that, on the contrary, this article can be construed that for regions that have received electricity services, the government and regional government could give opportunity to region-owned enterprises, private business entities, or cooperatives to provide electricity in a separate manner (unbundling).f	Article 11 (2) of the 2009 Electricity Law provides that the state-owned enterprise has the main priority for electricity supply business for public purposes. The role of private entities, cooperation and maintaining a self-reliant community, is to increase the supply of electricity to improve the electricity supply to the people.h
	4. In the event that there are no region-owned enterprises, private business entities, or cooperatives that can provide electricity in the respective area, the government is obliged to assign state-owned enterprises to supply electricity.	• The petitioners argue that, on the contrary, this article can be construed that if there is a region-owned enterprise, private business enterprise or cooperatives that can provide electricity in the respective areas, the government is not obliged to assign the state-owned enterprise to provide electricity.g	
3.	**Article 20** An electricity supply business license, as referred to in Article 19 paragraph (1) letter *a*, is stipulated in accordance with the type of business as referred to in Article 10 paragraph (1).	• The substance of this article is the same with the 2002 Electricity Law which separated the electricity business supply must be carried out by different legal entities, resulting in in vertical and horizontal unbundling.i • The horizontal unbundling will create disadvantages to PLN since each province will have a different regional budget that includes the electricity operational budget therein. This will create a deficit in the operational budget to cover the condition in each region by increasing the electricity sale price in each province and city.j	• MK considered that the petitioner cannot prove that this article is not in line with the Indonesian Constitution; MK did not provide further consideration for this article.k

continued on next page

Table A3.3: *continued*

No.	Article	Petitioner's Arguments	MK Consideration	MK Decision
4.	**Article 33**	The petitioners argue that this price stipulation mechanism is not in accordance with Article 33 of the Indonesian Constitution which emphasizes the social welfare aspect based on following arguments:	• The electricity sale price and electricity system lease under these market mechanisms are still subject to further approval of the government and regional government. This enables the government to subsidize the consumer with low purchasing power; therefore, this provision still observes the social welfare aspect under Article 33 of the Indonesian Constitution.[1]	
	1. The electricity sale price and the electricity system lease are stipulated based on fair business principles. Government or regional governments, in accordance with their respective authority, gives approval for the selling price of electricity and electricity system lease.	• Using the market price as the electricity sale price basis will make the petitioners suffer from an uncontrollable electricity price since it is based on market mechanism. • The government and regional governments do not have the role to intervene with this market mechanism and therefore the petitioners are suffering in a weaker position compared to business actors.		

continued on next page

Table A3.3:   *continued*

5.

Article 56

1. PT Perusahaan Listrik Negara (Persero) as a state-owned enterprise, formed based on Government Regulation Number 23 of 1994 regarding The Transformation of State Electricity Public Company to Become a Company (Persero)" is considered to have a electricity supply business license.

2. Within a maximum period of 2 years, the government shall have made the arrangements and stipulations of the electricity supply business license to state-owned enterprises as referred to in point 1 to be in accordance with the provisions of this law.

These articles mean that within 2 years, PLN shall apply for an electricity business license according to the types of business and shall be treated the same as the other electricity company.[m] This will require PLN to restructure its business which may result in employee termination.[n]

MK considered that the petitioner cannot prove as to how this article is not in line with the Indonesian Constitution; MK did not provide further consideration for these articles.[o]

continued on next page

Table A3.3: *continued*

No.	Article	Petitioner's Arguments	MK Consideration	MK Decision
4.	Within a maximum period of 2 years, the implementation of an Electricity Business Permit for Public Purposes, an Electricity Business License for Private Purposes, and an Electricity Supporting Business License Electricity to be issued based on the Law No. 15 of 1985 regarding electricity as referred to in number 3 shall be adjusted to be in accordance with the provisions of this law.			

MK = Mahkamah Konstitusi (Constitutional Court), PLN = Perusahaan Listrik Negara (State-Owned Electricity Enterprises).

a Government of Indonesia, Constitutional Court. 2009. Decision No. 149/PUU-VII/2009. Jakarta. p. 14, point (c) & (d).
b Footnote a, p. 91, point 2 & 3.
c Footnote a, p. 16.
d Footnote a, p. 96, point 3.12.
e Footnote a, p. 95, point (d).
f Footnote a, p. 14, point (e).
g Footnote a, p. 14, point (e).
h Footnote a, p. 95, point (c).
i Footnote a, p. 17.
j Footnote a, p. 17.
k Footnote a, p. 96, point 3.13.
l Footnote a, p. 96, point (e).
m Footnote a, p. 19, point c.
n Footnote a, p. 96, point 3.13.
o p. 96, pt. 3.13, Decision 149.

Source: Authors, based on MK's Decision 149.

Decision 111

With respect to the judicial review petition, MK substantially issues the following decisions:

- Article 10 (2) is conditionally unconstitutional and shall have no binding power if it is construed to allow electricity supply businesses to be run on an unbundled basis where there is no state control over the relevant unbundled services.

Article 11 (1) is conditionally unconstitutional and shall have no binding power if it is construed to mean that the principle of "controlled by the state" is not a requirement of applying the participation of these stated entities (i.e. including private entities) in the electricity supply business.

Below is the table on summary of Decision 111.

Table A3.4:   Summarizes Decision 111

No.	Article	Petitioner's Arguments	MK Consideration	MK Decision
1.	Article 10 (2) Electricity supply business for public purposes as referred to in paragraph (1) can be carried out in an integrated manner.	• The term "can be carried out in integrated manner" opens the possibility of the provision of electricity to be done in a non–integrated manner (unbundled) to result in 1. vertical unbundling, which is the separation of electricity business supply based on the types of business supply (transmission, distribution, generation, and sales) that can be carried out by different companies; and 2. horizontal unbundling, which is the regionalization of electricity business supply that can result in different electricity tariff in different regions.[b] • Electricity is a vital production sector to the state and shall only be controlled by the state (Article 33 of the Indonesian Constitution) where in this context, through PLN, as the legitimate state–owned entity, specifically designated to handle the electricity business supply for the people.[c] • Even though the central government still has control over electricity as set out in Article 5 (1) of the Electricity Law, the separation of electricity business sectors (unbundling) and the opening of electricity business to be carried out by private entities may result in the government's role to only become regulator and inspector since the control of electricity is carried out by private entities and not directly by the government.[d]	• MK's previous decision that rejected the judicial review of Article 10 (2) in Decision 149, cannot be construed as MK's acceptance toward the unbundling principle. The rejection was mainly based on MK's analysis, that unlike the provision in the 2002 Electricity Law that clearly stated that electricity supply business shall be conducted separately by different business entities (unbundling), Article 10 (2) of the 2009 Electricity Law does not apply such an unbundling principle in the electricity business supply for public purposes.[a] However, if in practice there are parties that construed Article 10 (2) of 2009 Electricity Law differently other than MK's interpretation, then Article 10(2) of 2009 Electricity Law is conditionally unconstitutional and shall have no binding power if it is construed to allow electricity supply businesses to be run on an unbundled basis where there is no state control over the relevant unbundled services.[e]	• MK grants some parts of the petitions, which are • stating that Article 10 (2) of the 2009 Electricity Law is conditionally unconstitutional and shall have no binding power if it is construed to allow electricity supply business to be run on an unbundled basis where there is no state control over the relevant unbundled services and • stating that Article 11 (1) of the 2009 Electricity Law is conditionally unconstitutional and shall have no binding power if it is construed to allow electricity supply business to be run where there is no state control over the relevant services, and • rejects the rest of the petitioner's request.

continued on next page

continued on next page

Table A3.4:   *continued*

| 2. | **Article 11 (1)**
Electricity supply business for public interest as referred to in Article 10(1) shall be conducted by state-owned enterprises, region-owned enterprises, private entities, cooperatives, and self-reliant communities engaged in the field of electricity supply. | • The state's control concept under the Indonesian Constitution stipulates that only the central government and regional government can control the vital production sectors which affect the livelihood of the people; therefore, private entities, cooperatives, and self-reliant communities cannot engage in electricity supply for public purposes.[f]

• The inclusion of private entities and cooperatives to be able to act as an electricity supply business breach the provision of Article 33 of the Indonesian Constitution which stipulates that the control over electricity shall be given to PLN as the legitimate state-owned entity that shall provide the procurement of electricity.[g]

• Private entities, cooperatives, and self-reliant communities shall not be allowed to participate in the production sectors that are vital to the state and affect the livelihood of the majority of the people since this can decrease state's control over electricity.[h]

• The inclusion of region-owned entities as legitimate parties that can carry out electricity business supply may be construed as allowing such entity to be able to carry out electricity business supply independently without any cooperation with PLN.

• The region-owned entities may be able to carry electricity business supply for public purposes provided that PLN must be prioritized and shall be included in any procurement of electricity for public purposes.[i] | • There is no prohibition for the involvement of private entities, cooperatives, or self-reliant communities in the electricity business supply for public purposes provided that such involvement will not affect the state's control over the electricity.

• However, since Article 11 (2) of the 2009 Electricity Law does not explicitly stipulate the state's control in such involvement, Article 11 (2) is conditionally constitutional and shall have no binding power if it is construed to allow electricity supply businesses to be run without the state's control; this does not eliminate the possibility of involvement by private entities, region-owned entities, cooperatives, or self-reliant communities in electricity business supply. |

Table A3.4: *continued*

continued on next page

No.	Article	Petitioner's Arguments	MK Consideration
3.	**Article 16** An electricity supporting business as intended by Article 15 item (a) shall include a. electricity supply installation consultancy; b. electricity supply installation construction and performance; c. electricity installation checking and testing; d. electricity installation operation; e. electricity installation maintenance; f. research and development; g. education and training; h. power tools and equipment laboratory testing; i. electricity tools and equipment certification; j. electricity technician competency certification; or k. other service business directly associated with power supplies	• An electricity supporting business, as set out in Article 16 (1) (d) and Article 16 (1) (e) i.e. electricity installation operation and electricity installation maintenance, shall not be included under the classification of electricity supporting businesses.[j] • Such inclusion may result in the termination of PLN's employee due to (i) the type of business being outsourced to third–party (ii) the establishment of other subsidiaries to conduct the operation and maintenance of power operation, regardless of the ownership status of the subsidiaries that are still under PLN's control.[k] • Therefore, the application of the 2009 Electricity Law may affect the petitioners' right over jobs and decent live under Article 27 (2) and Article 28D (2) of the Indonesian Constitution due to the establishment of PLN's new branch and cooperation with third–parties that result in the reduction of the role and jobs of the PLN's employee.[l]	• The classification of a business under this article does not necessarily mean that it is breaching Article 27 (2) and Article 28D (2) of the Indonesian Constitution since determination of jobs in PLN is highly subject to various factors including the job vacancy in the business. Therefore this cannot be applied generally and universally.[m] • MK also considers that this article does not contain any discriminative purposes to eliminate the people's rights over (a) job; therefore, MK opines that the petitioner's argument regarding the constitutionality of Article 16 (1) (d) & Article 16 (1) (e) is not legally reasonable.[n]

Table A3.4: *continued*

4.	**Article 33 (1)** The electricity sale price and the electricity system lease are determined based on fair business principles.	• This article adopted the fair business principle which is a market-oriented principle that fully relies on supply and demand. Such principle contains the neoliberalism idea (i.e. transfer control of economic sectors from public to private) which does not reflect the economic concept in Article 33(4) of the Indonesian Constitution which states that the national economy shall be based on a democratic economy upholding the principles of solidarity, efficiency along with fairness, sustainability, keeping the environment in perspective, and self-sufficiency.[o]	• The definition of electricity sale price includes all the costs which relate to the sales of the electricity generation; therefore, in determining the electricity sale price, it is impossible to dismiss and not take into account all the costs which related to the electricity sales and generation. MK stated that there is no legal uncertainty in this article.
5.	**Article 34 (5)** The electricity tariff for the consumer as set out in paragraph (1) and paragraph (2) can be set differently in each region within a business area.	• Electricity as a public utility and as a people's fundamental need shall be provided to the people with the same tariff and service; therefore, this article is breaching Article 28 (1) of the Indonesian Constitution that provides that everyone deserves equal treatment before law.[p] • This article alongside with Article 33 (1) above release the state's control over electricity price since electricity price determination is based on fair business principles, i.e., market-oriented without considering the people's purchasing power.[q]	• This provision must be read in entirety with the other paragraphs therein. Article 34 (5) of the 2009 Electricity Law set out that the electricity tariff must be stipulated by considering the balanced interests between national, regional, consumers, and business actors. • The regional interest in this context includes the regional economy and industry development; therefore, the purpose of this article is to provide fairness in stipulating the electricity sale price, particularly for the underdeveloped regions with low purchasing power. Where, in contrary, it will be unfair to stipulate the same tariff for the underdeveloped regions and other regions that are relatively more developed.[r]

continued on next page

Table A3.4:   *continued*

No.	Article	Petitioner's Arguments	MK Consideration	MK Decision
			• Applying fair business principles does not mean solely implementing a market-oriented principle. The whole context of this article is to emphasize that holders of electricity business licenses are prohibited from determining electricity prices without the government's approval (Article 34 (1) and Article 34 (2) 2009 Electricity Law).	
			• The criteria of fair business principles in this context refer to the stipulation of the determination of the tariff by the government, by taking into account the national and regional interests and economy development, not solely by the market.[s] Therefore, this is in accordance with the principle of a democratic economy in Article 33 of the Indonesian Constitution.	

continued on next page

Table A3.4:   *continued*

6.	**Article 56 (2)** Within a maximum period of 2 years, the government has made the arrangements and stipulations of the electricity supply business license to state-owned enterprises as referred to in paragraph (1) in accordance with the provisions of this Law.	PLN being one of the holders of electricity business license results in PLN no longer become the main controller of electricity supply.[t]	This article is a transitional provision which orders the government to conduct the arrangement and stipulation of electricity licenses to the state-owned entities within 2 years. This is not a breach of constitutional rights under the Indonesian Constitution.[u]

MK = Mahkamah Konstitusi (Institutional Court), PLN = Perusahaan Listrik Negara (State-Owned Electricity Company).

a Government of Indonesia, Constitutional Court. 2015. *Decision No. 111/PUU-XIII/2015*. Jakarta. page 106, point (b).
b Footnote a, p. 12.
c Footnote a, p. 34, point 5.
d Footnote a, p. 98, point (e).
e Footnote a, p. 106 – 107, point 1(b) & (c).
f Footnote a, p. 99 point 2(a).
g Footnote a, p. 99, point 2(d).
h Footnote a, para. 6.
i Footnote a, point 3.
j Footnote a, p. 45, point 5.
k Footnote a, point 7-9.
l Footnote a.
m Footnote a, p. 118.
n Footnote a.
o Footnote a, p. 40, point 5 & 6.
p Footnote a, p. 40, point 7 & 9.
q Footnote a, p. 88, para. 3.
r Footnote a, p. 114, point c.
s Footnote a, p. 115, point d.
t Footnote a, p. 99, point g.
u Footnote a, p. 108, point d.

Source: Authors, based on MK's Decision 111.

Appendix 4:
Relevant Regulations Regarding Electricity

1. Constitution of Republic of Indonesia of 1945 (Indonesian Constitution)

2. Law No. 22 of 2001 on Oil and Gas (Oil and Gas Law)

3. Law No. 20 of 2002 on Electricity Business (2002 Electricity Law)

4. Law No. 7 of 2004 on Water Resources (Water Law)

5. Law No. 30 of 2009 on Electricity Business (2009 Electricity Law)

6. Law No. 12 of 2011 on Establishment of Laws and Regulations (Law 12/2011)

7. Law No. 21 of 2014 on Geothermal (Geothermal Law)

8. Government Regulation No. 57 of 2001 on National Consumer Protection Agency (GR 57/2001)

9. Government Regulation No. 53 of 2004 on Electricity Market Supervisory Agency (GR 53/2003)

10. Government Regulation No. 14 of 2012 as amended by Government Regulation No. 23 of 2014 on Electricity Supply Business (GR 14/2012)

11. Government Regulation No. 62 of 2012 on Electricity Support Service Business (GR 62/2012)

12. Government Regulation No. 42 of 2012 on Cross-Border Sale and Purchases (GR 42/2012)

13. Government Regulation No 79 of 2014 on the National Energy Policy (GR 79/2014)

14. Government Regulation No. 24 of 2018 on Online Single Submission (OSS) Services (GR 24/2018)

15. Government Regulation No. 35 of 2009 as amended by Government Regulation No. 50 of 2016 on State Capital Participation of Indonesia in The Establishment of State-Owned Enterprises (Persero) in the Infrastructure Guarantee Sector (GR 35/2009)

16. Presidential Decree No. 104 of 2003 on The Sale Prices of Electricity of 2004 Provided by PLN (PD 103/2003)

17. Presidential Decree No. 37 of 1992 as amended by PD No. 38 of 1998 (PD 37/1992)

18. Presidential Regulation No. 90 of 2007 on Capital Investment Coordinating Board (PR 90/2007)

19. Presidential Regulation No. 86 of 2007 on Statistics Regulatory Body (PR 86/2007)

20. Presidential Regulation No. 38 of 2015 on Cooperation Between Government and Business Entities in Infrastructure Provision (PR 38/2015)

21. Presidential Regulation No. 75 of 2014 on Acceleration of Priority Infrastructure as amended by PR 122 of 2016 (PR 75/2014)

22. Presidential Regulation No. 9 of 2013 on the Management of Upstream Oil and Gas Activities (PR 9/2013)

23. Presidential Regulation No. 4 of 2016 on the Acceleration of the Construction of Electricity Infrastructure as amended by PR No. 14 of 2017 (PR 4/2016)

24. Presidential Regulation No. 71 of 2006 on the Assignment of PT Perusahaan Listrik Negara (Persero) to Conduct Development Acceleration of Electric Power Plant Using Coal as amended by PR No. 193 Of 2014 (PR 71/2006)

25. Presidential Regulation No. 72 of 2006 on Coordination Team of the Acceleration of Electric Power Plant as amended by PR No. 6 Of 2010 (PR 72/2006)

26. Presidential Regulation No. 22 of 2017 on the National General Energy Plan (PR 22/2007)

27. Presidential Regulation No. 71 of 2012 on the Implementation of Land Procurement for Public Interest Development as amended by PR No. 40/2014, PR No. 99/2014, PR No. 30/2015, and PR No. 148/2015 (PR 71/2012)

28. Presidential Regulation No. 4 of 2010 on the Assignment to PLN to Accelerate the Development of Power Plants using Renewable Energy, Coal and Gas as amended by PR 48/2011 (PR 4/2010)

29. Minister of Agrarian Affairs and Spatial Layout/Chairman of the National Land Agency No. 14 of 2018 on Location Permit (MoA 14/2018)

30. Minister of Energy and Mineral Resources Regulation No. 10 of 2017 on the Principles of Power Purchase Agreements (MEMR 10/2017)

31. Minister of Energy and Mineral Resources Regulation No. 49 of 2017 on the first amendment of MEMR 10/2017 (MEMR 49/2017)

32. Minister of Energy and Mineral Resources Regulation No. 10 of 2018 on the second amendment of (MEMR 10/2018)

33. Minister of Energy and Mineral Resources Regulation No. 1 of 2006 on Electrical Power Purchasing and/or Rental of Transmission Lines as amended by MEMR 4/2007 (MEMR 1/2006)

34. Minister of Energy and Mineral Resources Regulation No 2 of 2006 on Medium-Scale Business of Electricity Generation Using Renewable Energy (MEMR 2/2006)

35. Minister of Energy and Mineral Resources Regulation No. 5 of 2009 on Guidelines for Power Purchase by PLN from Cooperatives or other Business Entities (MEMR 5/2009)

36. Minister of Energy and Mineral Resources Regulation No. 28 of 2012 on Procedures for Applying Electricity Provision Business Area for Public Interests as amended by MEMR 7/2016 (MEMR 28/2012)

37. Minister of Energy and Mineral Resources Regulation No. 29 of 2012 on Capacity of Power Plant for Own Us Based on Operating Permit (MEMR 29/2012)

38. Minister of Energy and Mineral Resources Regulation No. 15 of 2010 on List of Accelerated Development Projects for the Development of Power Plant Using Renewable Energy, Coal and Gas and Related Transmissions as amended by MEMR No. 1 of 2012 (MEMR 15/2010)

39. Minister of Energy and Mineral Resources Regulation No. 35 of 2014 on The Delegation of Authority for the Issuance of Electricity Business Licenses in the Context of the Implementation of Integrated Single Window Services to the Chairman of the Investments Coordinating Board (MEMR 35/2014)

40. Minister of Energy and Mineral Resources Regulation No. 1 of 2017 on Parallel Operation of Power Plants with The Power Grids of PLN (MEMR 1/2017)

41. Minister of Energy and Mineral Resources Regulation No.48 of 2017 on the Supervision on Business Activities in Energy and Mineral Resources Sector (MEMR 48/2017)

42. Minister of Energy and Mineral Resources Regulation No.50 of 2017 on the Use of Renewable Energy for the Provision of Electricity (MEMR 50/2017)

43. Minister of Energy and Mineral Resources Regulation No. 19 of 2017 on The Use of Coal for Power Plants and Purchase of Excess Power (MEMR 19/2017)

44. Minister of Energy and Mineral Resources Regulation No. 1 of 2015 on Joint Cooperation in The Provision of Electricity and Joint Utilization of Electricity Network (MEMR 1/2015)

45. Minister of Energy and Mineral Resources Regulation No. 35 of 2013 as amended by Regulation No. 12 of 2016 on the Procedure for Obtaining Permits for Electric Power Business (MEMR 35/2013)

46. Minister of Energy and Mineral Resources Regulation No. 17 of 2014 regarding Purchase of Electricity from Geothermal Power (MEMR 17/2014)

47. Minister of Energy and Mineral Resources Regulation No. 19 of 2017 on The Use of Coal for Power Plants and Purchase of Excess Power (MEMR 19/2017)

48. Minister of Energy and Mineral Resources Regulation No. 15 of 2016 as amended by MEMR No. 13/2017 on Provision of Quick Service within 3 hours related to Infrastructure in the Energy and Natural Resources Sector (MEMR 15/2016)

49. Minister of Energy and Mineral Resources Regulation No. 5 of 2014 on Procedure of Accreditation and Certification for Electricity as amended by MEMR Regulation No. 10 of 2016 (MEMR 5/2014)

50. Minister of Energy and Mineral Resources Regulation No. 39 of 2018 on the Electronic Integrated Business Licensing Services in The Electricity Sector (MEMR 39/2018)

51. Minister of Finance Regulation No. 130/PMK.08/2016 on the Procedure of Government Guarantee Implementation for the Acceleration of Electricity Infrastructure Development (MOF 130/2016)

52. Minister of Finance Regulation 101/PMK.08/2018 on Procedures for Granting and Implementing the Joint Government Guarantee or Through Infrastructure Guarantee Business Entity (Badan Usaha Penjamin Infrastruktur/BUPI) On Risk of Failure to Pay from SOE Which Conduct Loans and / Or Issuance of Bonds for Infrastructure Financing (MOF 101/2018)

53. Minister of Industry Regulation 54/M-IND/PER/3/2012 regarding the Guidelines on the Use of Domestic Products for The Construction of Electricity Infrastructure as amended by MOI No. 05/M-IND/PER/2/2017

54. Head of BKPM Regulation No. 6 of 2018 on Guidelines and Procedures for the Implementation of Capital Investment Licensing and Facilities (BKPM Reg 6/2018)

55. Head of BKPM Regulation No. 7 of 2018 on Guidelines and Procedures for Capital Investment Implementation Monitoring (BKPM Reg 7/2018)

References

Alfian. 2010. PLN Labor Union to Challenge New Law on Electricity. The Jakarta Post. 20 January. http://www.thejakartapost.com/news/2010/01/20/pln-labor-union-challenge-new-law-electricity.html

Alliance for Rural Electrification. 2014. *Mini-grid Policy Toolkit–Policy and Business Frameworks for Successful Mini-grid Roll-outs*. https://www.ruralelec.org/sites/default/files/inensus-toolkit-en-21x21-web-ok.pdf

Capital Investment Coordinating Board (BKPM). Main Duty and Functions. https://www.bkpm.go.id/en/about-bkpm/bkpm-main-duty-and-function.

Bundesnetzagentur. Establishing Requirements. https://www.netzausbau.de/EN/requirements/en.html

Council of European Energy Regulators. 2016. *Status Review on Implementation of TSO and DSO Unbundling Provisions (Version 1.1)*. https://www.ceer.eu/en/eer_activities/all_regulatory_authority_decisions/-/asset_publisher/i9pPDyijR3Ht/document/id/6671175?inheritRedirect=false&redirect=https%3A%2F%2Fwww.ceer.eu%3A443%2Fen%2Feer_activities%2Fall_regulatory_authority_decisions%3Fp_p_id%3D101_INSTANCE_i9pPDyijR3Ht%26p_p_lifecycle%3D0%26p_p_state%3Dnormal%26p_p_mode%3Dview%26p_p_col_id%3Dcolumn-1%26p_p_col_pos%3D51%26p_p_col_count%3D54.

Energy Policy Research Group. 2014. *Global Trends in Electricity Transmission System Operation: Where does the future lie?* https://www.eprg.group.cam.ac.uk/wp-content/uploads/2014/01/Draft-Working-Paper-MC.pdf.

F. Seymour and A. Sari. 2002. Indonesia: Electricity Reform under Economic Crisis. In N. Dubash, ed. Power Politics, Equity and Environment in Electricity Reform. Washington, DC: World Resources Institute.

Government of Brazil, Energy Research Office. 2018. *Brazilian Electricity Auctions in 2018–Presenting the results and how they influence energy planning studies*. http://epe.gov.br/sites-en/sala-de-imprensa/noticias/Documents/Informe%20Leil%C3%B5es%202018_English_FINAL.pdf.

Government of Indonesia. 1960. *Law No. 6 concerning Census*. Jakarta.

Government of Indonesia. 1960. *Law No. 7 concerning Statistics*. Jakarta.

Government of Indonesia. 1985. *Law No. 15 concerning electricity*. Jakarta.

Government of Indonesia. 1991. *Presidential Decree No. 39 concerning Overseas Commercial Loan Management Coordination*.

Government of Indonesia. 1999. *Law No. 36 concerning Telecommunication.* Jakarta.

Government of Indonesia. 2002. *Law No. 20 concerning Electricity.* Jakarta

Government of Indonesia. 2003. *Government Regulation No. 53 concerning Electricity Market Supervisory Agency.* Jakarta

Government of Indonesia, Constitutional Court. 2003. *Decision No. 001-021-022/PUU-1/2003.* Jakarta.

Government of Indonesia, Ministry of Commmunication. 2003. *Decree No. 31 concerning the Determination of Indonesian Telecommunication Regulatory Body.* Jakarta.

Government of Indonesia. 2004. *Law No. 38 concerning Road.* Jakarta.

Government of Indonesia. 2005. *Government Regulation No. 15 concerning Toll Toad.* Jakarta.

Government of Indonesia, Ministry of Public Works and Housing. 2005. *Ministerial Regulation No. 295/PRT/M/2005 concerning Toll Road Regulatory Agencies.* Jakarta

Government of Indonesia. 2007. *Presidential Regulation No. 86 on Statistics Indonesia.* Jakarta.

Government of Indonesia. 2009. *Law No. 30 concerning Electricity.* Jakarta.

Government of Indonesia, Constitutional Court. 2009. *Decision No. 149/PUU-VII/2009.* Jakarta.

Government of Indonesia. 2011. *Law No. 12 concerning the Formulation of Laws and Regulations.* Jakarta.

Government of Indonesia, Ministry of Energy and Mineral Resources. 2012. *Decree No. 3155 concerning Transfer of Duties, Functions and Organizations in the Implementation of Upstream Oil and Gas Business Activities.* Jakarta.

Government of Indonesia, Ministry of Energy and Mineral Resources. 2012. *Decree No. 3156 concerning Transfer of Oil and Gas Upstream Business Activities Operational Agency (BP Migas) Employees.* Jakarta

Government of Indonesia. 2014. *Presidential Regulation No. 87 concerning the implementing regulation for Law No. 12/2011.* Jakarta.

Government of Indonesia, Constitutional Court. 2015. *Decision No. 111/PU-XIII/2015.* Jakarta.

Government of Indonesia, Ministry of Energy and Mineral Resources. 2015. *RUKN 2015.* Jakarta. http://www.djk.esdm.go.id/pdf/Draft%20RUKN/Draft%20RUKN%202015%20-%202034.pdf.

Government of Indonesia, Ministry of Energy and Mineral Resources. 2018. *RUPTL 2018.* Jakarta. http://www.djk.esdm.go.id/pdf/RUPTL/Salinan%20Sesuai%20Aslinya_Kepmen%20ESDM%20ttg%20Pengesahan%20RUPTL%20PT%20PLN%20(Persero)%202018-2027.pdf.

Government of Indonesia. 2018. *Presidential Regulation No. 36 concerning the Management of Upstream Oil and Gas Activities.* Jakarta

Government of Indonesia, Ministry of Commmunication. 2018. *Decree No. 15 concerning the amendmen of Decree No. 31/2003 concerning the Determination of Indonesian Telecommunication Regulatory Body.* Jakarta.

Government of Kosovo, Energy Regulatory Office. 2007. *ETR2–Allowed Revenues Calculation Guidance.* http://ero-ks.org/Price%20and%20Tariffs/Price%20and%20tariffs%202007/Price%20and%20Tariffs%2016_10_07/ETR2_Allowed_Revenues_Calculation_Guidance_eng.pdf.

Government of Kosovo, Energy Regulatory Office. 2007. *Annual Report.* http://ero-ks.org/Raportet-Vjetore/English/Annual_Report_2007.pdf

Government of Kosovo, Energy Regulatory Office. 2012. *The Sixth Electricity Tariff Review (ETR6) (2012–2013).* http://ero-ks.org/Tarifat/2012/Feb/KEK_Consultation_Paper.pdf.

Government of Kosovo, Energy Regulatory Office. 2012. *Annual Report.* http://ero-ks.org/Annual%20Report/Annual%20Report%202012/Raporti_Vjetor_2012_ZRRE_eng.pdf

Government of Nigeria, Nigerian Electricity Regulatory Commission. 2006. *Requirements for licenses to be granted pursuant to the application for licenses regulations, 2006.* https://www.nercng.org/index.php/library/documents/Licensing/Requirements-for-Licencing/.

Government of Nigeria, Nigerian Electricity Regulatory Commission. 2010. *Regulation No: NERC-R-0110A on the Application for Licenses (Generation, Transmission, System Operations, Distribution & Trading).* http://nercng.org/nercdocs/Regulation-for-the-Application-for-Licence.pdf

Indonesia Infrastructure Guarantee Fund. *Company History and Milestones.* Jakarta. http://www.iigf.co.id/en/about-pt-pii/company-history.

International Renewable Energy Agency. 2018. *Insights on Planning for Power System Regulators.* https://irena.org/-/media/Files/IRENA/Agency/Publication/2018/Jun/IRENA_Insights_on_planning_2018.pdf.

IPP Office South Africa. 2019. *Independent Power Producer Procurement Programme.* https://www.ipp-projects.co.za/Home/About

J. Asshiddiqie. 2006. *Perkembangan dan Konsolidasi Lembaga Negara Pasca Reformasi.* Jakarta: Penerbit Sekretariat Jenderal dan Kepaniteraan Mahkamah Konstitusi RI.

MT Sambodo. 2016. From Darkness to Light. Singapore: ISEAS Publishing.

Organisation for Economic Co-operation and Development. 2014. *OECD Best Practice Principles for Regulatory Policy: The Governance of Regulators.* http://dx.doi.org/10.1787/9789264209015-en.

PT Sarana Multi Infrastruktur. About Us. https://www.ptsmi.co.id/about-us/who-we-are/

PwC. 2018. *Power in Indonesia – Investment and Taxation Guide 2018*. https://www.pwc.com/id/en/publications/assets/eumpublications/utilities/power-guide-2018.pdf.

State of Georgia. 1991. *Georgia Code Title 46 Public Utilities and Public Transportation*. https://codes.findlaw.com/ga/title-46-public-utilities-and-public-transportation/#!tid=N78181DC0BE9211DAAC5F876AC7189607

The Brattle Group. 2014. *Competition in Transmission Planning and Development: Current Status and International Experience*. http://files.brattle.com/system/publications/pdfs/000/004/977/original/competition_in_transmission_planning_and_development.pdf?1391196850.

The Committee for the Acceleration of Prioritized Infrastructure Development (KPPIP). *Composition and Organizational Structure*. Jakarta. https://kppip.go.id/en/about-kppip/composition-and-organizational-structure-of-kppip/.

World Bank Group Public–Private Partnership Legal Resource Center. 1998. *Concessions for infrastructure–A guide to their design and award*. https://ppp.worldbank.org/public-private-partnership/sites/ppp.worldbank.org/files/ppp_testdumb/documents/concessions_fulltoolkit.pdf.

World Bank. 2018. *Infrastructure Sector Assessment Program–Indonesia*. Washington, DC.